From Charity to Change

FROM CHARITY TO CHANGE

Inside the World
of Canadian Foundations

Hilary M. Pearson

McGill-Queen's University Press
Montreal & Kingston • London • Chicago

ISBN 978-0-2280-1450-8 (cloth)
ISBN 978-0-2280-1559-8 (ePDF)
ISBN 978-0-2280-1560-4 (ePUB)

Legal deposit fourth quarter 2022
Bibliothèque nationale du Québec

Printed in Canada on acid-free paper that is 100% ancient forest free
(100% post-consumer recycled), processed chlorine free

Funded by the   Financé par le
Government   gouvernement
of Canada   du Canada

Canada Council   Conseil des arts
for the Arts   du Canada

We acknowledge the support of the Canada Council for the Arts.

Nous remercions le Conseil des arts du Canada de son soutien.

Library and Archives Canada Cataloguing in Publication

Title: From charity to change : inside the world of Canadian foundations / Hilary M. Pearson.

Names: Pearson, Hilary M., author.

Description: Includes bibliographical references and index.

Identifiers: Canadiana (print) 20220265712 | Canadiana (ebook) 20220265844 |
    ISBN 9780228014508 (cloth) | ISBN 9780228015598 (ePDF) | ISBN 9780228015604 (ePUB)

Subjects: LCSH: Family foundations – Canada. | LCSH: Endowments – Canada. |
    LCSH: Charities – Canada.

Classification: LCC HV105 .P43 2022 | DDC 361.7/6320971 – dc23

This book was designed and typeset by Peggy & Co. Design in 11/14 Adobe Garamond Pro.

For Katharine
A gifted giver, much missed

Contents

Tables and Figures

Tables

Figures

Acknowledgments

While writing this book, I spoke to many committed and thoughtful people who are engaged in the work of Canadian philanthropy as funders, partners, observers, and supporters. I owe a great debt to the leaders of the foundations whose stories are told in this book. They were unstintingly generous with their time, and they provided depth and context to the work of their foundations. My sincere thanks go to Jehad Aliweiwi, Naomi Azrieli, Ian Boeckh, Amy Buskirk, Sherry Campbell, Jean-Marc Chouinard, Sophie de Caen, Sandy Houston, Marcel Lauzière, Bruce Lawson, Valerie Lemieux, Bruce Lourie, Laura Manning, Elizabeth McIsaac, Helen McLean, Jenn Miller, Andrew Molson, Colette Murphy, Alan Northcott, Lili-Anna Pereša, Claude Pinard, Llewellyn and Susan Smith, Eric St-Pierre, Sylvie Trottier, Bob Wyatt, and Sadia Zaman. I am very grateful to the wise colleagues who took time to comment on earlier drafts: Tim Brodhead, Stephen Huddart, and Michael Alberg-Seberich. And I am thankful for the insights of many who are innovators and contributors to the future of Canadian philanthropy: Liban Abokor, Aatif Buskanderi, Raksha Bhayana, Wanda Brascoupé, and Victoria Grant. I acknowledge the support of Philanthropic Foundations Canada and, in particular, my former colleague Liza Goulet, who cheerfully and meticulously provided me with detailed data on the private foundation sector in Canada. This book is dedicated to my sister Katharine, former director, Social Innovation Generation at the McConnell Foundation, who was my inspiration for exploring the innovative work of McConnell and so many other Canadian foundations. Finally, I want to express my greatest gratitude to my husband and daughter, who have loyally supported, constructively criticized, and always strongly encouraged my curiosity and enthusiasm for the work of Canadian foundations. They make all possible.

From Charity to Change

Introduction

What Is Philanthropy For?

Who are Canada's private foundations? These largely unknown but power-ful philanthropic organizations are important to many communities. They fund charities across Canada working on a wide range of issues. Why don't we know more about them? Shouldn't we have more information about who they are and how they decide to spend their money? And shouldn't we have a better idea of what difference they make?

On a cold afternoon in November 2001, I sat with four private foun-dation leaders at a polished boardroom table in a downtown Montreal office tower. I was there for a job interview. The foundation leaders were looking for someone to head a new association for foundations in Canada. It was a world I frankly knew little about. I had been working in the non-profit sector as a consultant and policy adviser to boards of directors and staff leaders of non-profits. But I had never approached any foundations directly, and I knew few by name. As a Montrealer, I did have a sense of the importance of private foundations to the city where I lived. Named after prominent donors familiar in Canadian business history, such as Molson, Bronfman, Webster, McConnell, Bombardier, or Coutu, these long-established foundations were generous givers to many institutions in the city. They had contributed, over the twentieth century, to the major educational, health, and cultural institutions of Montreal: McGill University, the Montreal Neurological Institute-Hospital, the Université de Montreal, the YMCAs of Quebec, the McCord Museum, the Montreal General Hospital, the Montreal Children's Hospital, and more. I also knew that new families were joining the foundation world. In 2000, a year before I walked into that boardroom, one of the wealthiest families in Quebec, the Chagnon family, had created Canada's largest family foundation.[1] So I understood that this was an influential and still growing set of players.

On the other hand, I also knew the public had mixed views about private foundations and the wealthy people who created them. Canadians might think approvingly of private foundations as generous funders; more negatively, some think private foundations pursue vanity projects of interest only to their donors. In the 1990s, when the media reported occasionally on the work of private foundations, they focused on the wealth of the donors or that they were receiving public tax breaks for their generosity. Where their name was being added to a building or program, the story might be about the gilding of their reputation. But there was no nuance to these stories. I believed the story of private foundations was more complicated and more interesting. However, I realized I didn't have enough human details to counter the skeptics. In that moment in late 2001, I couldn't provide specific examples of the work of private foundations that would lend support to the idea that they were much more than they seemed in the popular imagination. The foundation leaders around the table asked if I could make a compelling case to encourage more donors and families to set up a family foundation. They wanted to know how I, as leader of their new association, would persuade the government that it was worth investing public money in private foundations. This was a challenge. How could I argue that governments should provide tax incentives to wealthy Canadians who already have so much? Was there something uniquely important about private foundations that justified the public incentives for their creation? And why should donors think of setting up a foundation, particularly if it made them more visible and potentially exposed them to public criticism?

My curiosity was piqued. Although I couldn't yet make the case for them, I persuaded the foundation leaders that I could learn. Over the next two decades, as leader of their new association,[2] I worked with private and public foundations both small and large, in all parts of the country. And I had a chance to compare Canadian philanthropy with the large and influential American foundation sector, and with philanthropic organizations in the United Kingdom and continental Europe, as well as in Australia and New Zealand.

This book is my answer to the questions I asked myself in that job interview. And it is an argument for the unique value foundations create in our society. It begins with a deeper dive into the relatively unknown world of private foundations. The Canadian foundation world keeps a low profile. We know some of the famous names of American philanthropy – Ford, Rockefeller, Gates, and now Bezos and Scott – but names come much less readily to mind in Canada. As many foundation leaders have commented wryly, if you meet one foundation, you meet only *one* foundation. You certainly don't know much or more about *all* foundations. Each is as individual as its founding family or donor. Many foundations in Canada are reluctant to be visible in any way. In their view, "private" means "private." Although all registered charitable foundations must share information about their purposes and grants with the federal government as a condition of their registration, most are not publicly and proactively visible in the ways we have come to expect in the digital age.

Yet there are much deeper dimensions to private philanthropy than simple charity. Each foundation may be different in its own way. Nevertheless, we can connect their singular stories to a bigger story about the role foundations can play in our society, both present and future. In this book I give more life to this story by taking a closer look at the strategies of a specific group of Canadian private foundations. These funders have moved far beyond the approach of distributing grants in response to pleas from various charities, while keeping most of their funds passively locked into endowments and investment portfolios. The work of these foundations sets them apart. They have chosen to contribute actively to change – in our social systems, our public policies, and our economic structures. My intention is to illustrate their significance by describing why and how they act as they do, and how they think about their impact. Along the way I raise broader questions about the legitimacy of the private foundation model as we see it playing out in the changing context of the twenty-first century.

I want to focus on Canadian examples since little is known in any comprehensive way about Canadian foundations. Should we, in Canada, care about whether we have a visible and effective private foundation sector? What issues do the funding decisions of Canadian foundations raise for us as a society? There are many ways in which foundations act to change lives in their communities; is there something different about how Canadian foundations choose to do it? Can we identify a distinctive

Canadian philanthropy that is shaped by our history, which stretches back to pre-colonial times when the many First Nations and Inuit peoples were sharing and helping each other in relations of reciprocity? Does modern philanthropy have a special role to play in helping us move as a country through the major transitions we face in the 2020s, not least of which is the adjustment to the climate emergency? As I answer these questions, I draw from thoughtful discussions and critiques of the role and work of private philanthropy in the United States and globally.

Private Philanthropy: From Benevolence to Social Change?

My starting point for understanding philanthropy in Canada is two-fold: the Indigenous world view of gifting relationships between individuals, communities, and previous and future generations, and the colonial view of philanthropy based largely on the centuries-old western European view of philanthropy as charity. This latter view treats philanthropy, at its core, as benevolence or goodwill toward others. In classical times, Greek and Roman civilizations of Europe considered philanthropy to be an affair of the wealthy. Judaic and Islamic traditions of *tzedakah*, *zakat*, and *sadaqah*[3] emphasized the communal aspects of charity and its importance in building solidarity and showing generosity toward the poor. As the Catholic Church spread across Europe, philanthropy borrowed from these traditions and became increasingly defined as a practice to alleviate the condition of the poor.[4] Whether wealthy or not, good Christians were expected to share what they had with those less fortunate. Church institutions, such as monasteries, convents, and parishes, became centres for both philanthropy and "hospitality," welcoming the weary travellers, and supporting the sick. This alms-giving concept of philanthropy was predominant for centuries in European societies.[5] The three Abrahamic religions and their attitude to the relationship between the rich and the poor shaped thinking about philanthropy in Canada in the centuries after colonization. In contrast, the Indigenous sharing traditions of gift exchanges "aren't merely about extending 'goodwill' but rather, simply, the way things are done in relationships."[6] This perspective was disregarded by non-Indigenous people for decades after colonial settlers arrived in Canada but was never lost by Indigenous communities and is now beginning to re-emerge as Canadian philanthropy begins to recognize its commitment and obligation to reconciliation. Yet this is a recent change as I discuss in a later chapter. The world of Canadian foundations today remains very much based on a western concept of philanthropic practice.

Over time, as the influence of religion receded in post-colonial Canada, the notion of charity was combined with, and even overtaken by, the goal of improving the conditions of society for all, not just the poor. Private philanthropists began to create trusts or foundations as a vehicle for assembling funds to support their giving to public charities serving the less fortunate and to improve the lives of all their fellow community members. Foundations and trusts became vehicles for the "betterment of society." Donors created endowed funds to support the development of community institutions serving the public good, such as universities, colleges, hospitals, museums, and other arts bodies. Well-known American examples are Andrew Carnegie's funding of public libraries across North America or John D. Rockefeller's funding of the building of the University of Chicago. In Canada in the 1930s, the Montreal businessman Jack McConnell, influenced by Rockefeller's example, set up a trust to fund capital improvements at McGill University in Montreal. This eventually became the McConnell Foundation, the second-oldest established family foundation in Canada,[7] preceded only by the foundation of the Massey family, manufacturers of agricultural equipment, created in Toronto in 1918,[8] which funded the construction of Toronto landmark institutions such as Massey Hall and Hart House at the University of Toronto.

Charitable foundations today are structured individual givers. Their typical modern form is an endowed fund, using income from the invested capital to make grants to charities. This form of philanthropy is familiar because it receives public attention. The media regularly feature stories about multi-million-dollar foundation gifts to charities. They highlight the generosity of the giver and the act of giving itself. But media coverage rarely captures or conveys the phenomenon of *strategic* giving, oriented toward changing fundamental social or economic conditions. Telling this story is much more difficult. When a foundation decides to move beyond simple benevolence or institutional patronage to use its resources to address the causes, not just the symptoms, of social problems, it is taking on a more complex and less traditional role. In some cases, foundations may take public positions on – and advocate for – solutions that might represent radical shifts. Darren Walker, president of the Ford Foundation, captured the underlying concept of this approach eloquently in his 2019 book *From Generosity to Justice*: "When we move our work beyond generosity and toward justice, we can make not only meaningful differences in people's lives but also sustainable, structural change to benefit entire communities."[9] In speaking of its mission now, the Ford Foundation has adopted a language that focuses on dignity of all individuals, human rights, and equitable participation. It describes investing in "transformative ideas, individuals and institutions" and "re-imagining philanthropy to catalyze leaders and organizations driving social justice and building movements across the globe."[10] This is activist philanthropy indeed. And it is serving as a model for the work of other private foundations, in Canada as in the United States.

The Changing Narrative: From Investors to Partners

What motivates foundation leaders to redefine themselves from bestowers of charity to funders of change? When I began my work as leader of an association of foundations and took on the challenge of creating a compelling story about the work of private foundations, I tried to communicate a new version of their role, updated from the traditional guise of charitable funder to a seemingly more sophisticated description of foundation as social "investor." According to this story, private foundations, with their unrestricted funds and higher risk tolerance, can serve an important role as the "angel investors" of the non-profit sector. Like early-stage business investors, they can take on risk and fund the development of good ideas and models for social change by supporting research, experimentation, and demonstration pilots. I wrote in the preface to a 2003 collection of stories about philanthropic work, *Foundations Seeing the World Differently*,[11] that "foundations can support the untested, spot the unexplored, take risks on the unproven, and convene the players around major issues in their communities." Foundations as investors matter to society, I suggested, because they are willing to take the necessary risks to foster social innovation.

While some of this is valid, the investor model for philanthropy doesn't capture the reality of how social change is made. Private investors place a bet that there will be a way to scale up and profit as a new product or service becomes widely adopted and successful, and they usually want an exit strategy. In the Canadian social context, scaling up would mean governments are willing to take over and allow the social investor to exit. And it is not clear that government is the best vehicle for scouting or for adopting social innovations. Given fiscal deficits and pressures, as well as lack of innovation skills, governments at all levels are cautious about agreeing to initiate or to adopt social innovations. So the exit strategy to government funding isn't obvious for philanthropic investors.

One of the interesting questions to explore in relation to Canadian philanthropy is how the role of the state in Canada has affected the growth and strategies of foundations. Charitable trusts and foundations in Canada have been historically private, not public, in their nature. That is, they have been used by private individuals for their own philanthropic giving back to community, without reference to the public sector. As the Canadian state became ever more engaged from the 1960s on in building large-scale social support policies and programs, this may have heightened the reticence of foundation boards to engage in social transformation. Social change needs to be implemented democratically if it is to benefit the largest number of people. Foundations cannot and should not be the owners of social change. The idea of the controlling private investor does not fit with the concept of democratically driven change. Coupled with the relatively small size of private foundations in Canada, this reticence kept foundations from involving themselves in any major efforts to shape large-scale social change, even at early stages. They have been reluctant to act as backup funders for basic services even when government has withdrawn from funding them. They have shared in the public consensus that it is the mandate and obligation of democratically elected governments to act as the primary policy makers and redistributors to achieve greater social justice.

This does not mean foundations are or should be relegated to marginal players. Foundations in the 2020s are funding the discovery of new knowledge and seeding new ideas. They hope to influence public policy with the ideas they have funded. But for implementation, they are looking to other partners in their work: social enterprises, universities, even businesses. They are not assuming the public sector will act as the later-stage funder and implementor of these ideas. Instead, they are funding cross-sector platforms and social networks or movements to move these innovations forward. Government may or may not choose to engage in the work of these networks. But public sector engagement is not a precondition for philanthropic funding.

In my view, the respective roles of government and philanthropy should not be framed as "either/or" or as "first/later." Some suggest private philanthropy should be abolished and that the answer is for the state to tax and distribute wealth under democratic principles. Yet, the roles of governments and foundations can be complementary or even co-dependent. Inarguably, the state (government) is more accountable to the public in its distribution of public benefits. Yet philanthropy can play a role in holding the state accountable, in supporting and convening the unrepresented or those whose voices are not heard. Inarguably, government has more scope to deliver services on a broad scale and with resources that far outweigh private resources. Yet philanthropy can act to identify gaps and develop routes to access to services for those who are marginalized. Government can work across a whole social system. Philanthropy can pinpoint specific instances of innovation that can be grown locally and lead to greater impact at scale. In this frame, the role of private foundations is not simply to hand over the results of their risky investments in social change and exit, but to complement and amplify the redistributive efforts of elected public officials and administrators.

How else to tell the story of what foundations are doing, if the comparison to private sector angel investing is not quite accurate? In the mid-2000s, some foundations began to use the approach of so-called "strategic" philanthropy. Observers described this approach with a catchy term that blends philanthropy and business, "philanthrocapitalism."[12] In practice, this term has been applied more to American foundations, such as those started by wealthy technology billionaires in Silicon Valley. These foundations, often led by entrepreneurial living donors who have created, not inherited, their wealth, became more prominent in the United States as fortunes were made in information technology. They proactively chose their issues and approaches, developed "theories of change," and took on staff to work on solutions. They funded their own projects (or funded initiatives designed to their specifications by grantees). So-called strategic foundations were interested in determining and measuring specific outcomes and impacts. This had the merit of being more rigorous and disciplined around the work. But, as with the idea of the social investor, this approach was controlling. It did not open the way to more collaborative approaches, even if it was appealing for a foundation to run its own show. And it has not been characteristic of Canadian philanthropists.

The story of Canadian foundations isn't best told, in my view, through the individualized language of investing or business. It is better expressed through the language of partnership. Since the 2010s, an interest in changing power dynamics and relationships has led a handful of Canadian private foundations to begin moving away from making decisions behind their boardroom doors. They are beginning to place more trust in community organizations. Rather than asking for and evaluating grant proposals without external input, they are inviting community partners to work collaboratively on projects that will lead to social change. They might even commit to "trust-based" philanthropy, with unrestricted and open-ended funding of community partners. This is not an arms-length approach. Funders remain engaged as partners, building capacity where needed; convening, or helping to weave networks; and facilitating teams.

Part of the reason for this evolution to a more collaborative approach is the realization that the biggest challenges we face as a society are systemic and complex. Climate change; entrenched economic, social, and racial inequalities; and global pandemics are not resolved simply through mitigation of consequences. It takes mitigation of causes. Adaptation is needed. But prevention is also crucial. It takes everyone collectively to think and act effectively on these issues. To work in this way requires foundations to go beyond selecting what works (or has potential) and providing the financial resources for it, to bringing others together to share resources (including creativity and direct experience), and to using their voices to influence policy makers.

Foundations and the "Social Licence to Operate"

As foundations become more visible, community organizations, media commentators, analysts, and politicians can ask another uncomfortable question: What gives foundations the credibility, the right, to act as they do to change communities, sometimes in profound ways? This question takes on additional urgency in the 2020s, even more so as the consequences of the COVID-19 pandemic make clear the income disparities, social injustice, and lack of equity and economic inclusion in our country. I believe the interventions of philanthropy in the space between people, communities, businesses, and governments can be both legitimate and valuable. But in being active in this way, private philanthropy must also accept greater accountability for its power, and responsibility for managing that power more equitably in its interactions.

Private foundations must think carefully about their "social licence to operate" if they are going to withstand public scrutiny and increasingly angry critiques. The idea of the need for such a licence is not new. Wealth draws envy and philanthropy draws suspicion. The two are connected. Anonymous or completely altruistic giving may not attract much public attention. But the giving of large donors and large foundations is better known because there is value in recognizing it (for both recipient and donor) and/or because it must be made public by regulation. And this giving may be perceived as having strings attached. Or, if the gifts have an impact on communities or public policies, they may be perceived as attempts by the wealthy to exert power. In these cases, people may ask by what "right" do donors make these decisions that affect the lives of others? What is their legitimacy?

In the United States, observers across the media and in the academy are critiquing the role played by wealthy individuals and large foundations (whether new or long-established) in fundamentally important social and economic areas: education, health care, immigration, community development, the environment, and climate change. As many argue, critical interest is also being prompted, as in the earliest days of the twentieth century, by the great income inequality and power imbalances created by public choices about the relationship between state and business under capitalism. The critiques come from Americans because the imbalances are particularly striking in the United States. But the suspicion of philanthropy and its connection to private wealth crosses borders. In Canada, large individual donors and private foundations are less well-known and, therefore, their legitimacy is not challenged as frequently. Nevertheless, the question of the legitimacy of philanthropy is as relevant in Canada as it is south of our border, and the public critique has become more vociferous since the crisis of the pandemic.

Should private philanthropy rely for legitimacy in the public eye *only* on its compliance with government regulations? Historical experience and current criticism suggest there is an ethical and philosophical obligation to go beyond regulatory compliance. Foundations, particularly those that take on a mission for social change, should be mindful of social and public influence on, and expectations of, their behaviour. A private foundation must think of its legitimacy as both regulatory and normative. It is obligated not only by the state but by the expectations and needs of its grantees and partners. The key to legitimacy is to be willing to demonstrate accountability, which then builds public trust. This can be done through accountability to government regulators, *and* through transparency of goals, strategies, and evidence. Such transparency involves more open communication through exchanges with grantees and partners, and more public communication through websites, reports, and other forms of media. Not every foundation is going to create this kind of legitimacy for itself in the same way. The range of philosophies and operational strategies among private foundations means there is no single formula. The balance will be decided by the history, context, and operating style of each foundation.

Profiles in Canadian Philanthropy

In this book I explore how some Canadian foundations are examining their practices and working out their approaches to creating both more impact and greater accountability. The book is structured around the individual stories of a selected group of foundations. It is not a detailed history of philanthropy or foundations in Canada, nor does it cover the many types of foundations and philanthropic vehicles that exist in the country. It is told from my own perspective and my understanding of the work of a group of foundations, most of them private, that are trying new approaches, influencing others, and acting as partners in change. Through case studies, I explore their histories and motivations. I describe the work they are doing on current social and economic issues: adapting to climate change, building new relationships with Indigenous communities, integrating migrants and refugees, fostering access to education and mental health treatment for young people, developing new workforce development strategies, and strengthening cities and neighbourhoods. I describe how these foundations have shifted from acting as quiet individual funders to engaging in structured collaborations and catalyzing new movements and shared platforms. These are individualized stories, based on personal interviews with leaders and board members. They are told from the perspective of the funders themselves, and not from the perspective of their grantees and partners, although many of these foundations would insist their work depends on good listening to the perspectives and feedback from their partners. My goal is to provide a more nuanced and deeper narrative that shows how these foundations play their part in our social ecosystem.

Why is it important to write about this admittedly unrepresentative group of Canadian foundations? First, because they provide a window, of sorts, into the generally opaque world of Canadian philanthropy. There

have been many books written about American and European private
philanthropy by academics, journalists, and advisers. Some of these
books, such as *Just Giving* by Robert Reich, *Giving Done Well* by Phil
Buchanan, *Winners Take All* by Anand Giridharadas, and *Decolonizing
Wealth* by Edgar Villanueva have received much attention. Some have even
achieved bestseller status. In Europe, new thinking about the approaches
of private foundations is also giving visibility to the potential and power of
private philanthropy. Yet, up to now, there has been no book-length
account written by a single author about the work of individual Canadian
private foundations. Researchers, historians, and journalists have written
biographies or histories about Canadian business leaders and donors
such as J.W. McConnell, J.P. Bickell, and Samuel and Saidye Bronfman,
and the philanthropic foundations they created. And there is a growing
stream of papers and articles from academic researchers and foundation
observers who are examining the history and roles of Canadian foundations. A research centre, PhiLab at the Université du Québec à Montréal, is
sponsoring pan-Canadian academic research on the transformative role of
Canadian foundations in addressing social inequality and climate change.
The leaders of PhiLab have produced a multi-chapter compendium[13] by
several authors that includes chapters on the history and current role
of foundation philanthropy in Canada. Yet the literature on Canadian
foundations is still very limited.

A second reason for writing this book now is that its subject is of
interest to a much wider group than the private foundation community
itself: the founders, staff, and board members of the over six thousand
private foundations in Canada today. The work of philanthropy is important to understand for the leaders of non-profit organizations that are
funded by foundations, for public policy makers, for professional advisers
and students of foundation philanthropy, for corporate leaders with an
interest in social responsibility, and for leaders of organizations that create
and manage platforms and networks to link philanthropy to business,
government, and the community. These different audiences have a stake
in learning about how foundation philanthropy operates in Canada. And
the diversity of audiences is an indication of the wide scope and potential
impact of foundation players.

We need to understand more about the work of philanthropic foundations in Canada because they matter to the success of our society, to
its ability to sustain, include, and benefit all of us. Canadian private

foundations, by and large, have escaped the popular criticism that has been levelled at large American private foundations in waves for over a century. Suspicion of these foundations connects to an important and powerful story about inequality, the exploitations of colonialism and capitalism, and the arrogance of the super-rich. While we still have very few billionaire foundations in Canada, private foundations here, too, are beginning to be confronted by more direct accusations of lack of accountability and transparency, of arrogance in their funding decisions, and of antidemocratic elitism. Will they retreat into anonymity? Or will donors simply turn away from the option of creating private foundations? I would argue, as a critical friend, that foundations in Canada, as elsewhere, cannot take refuge in their invisibility and self-deprecation. In a stressed and unequal society, the wealth of endowed foundations is too easy a target. It is more important than ever, therefore, to tell an accurate story about why, what, and how foundations operate.

The Future of Canadian Foundation Philanthropy

The future for foundation philanthropy holds many unanswered questions. In the current landscape, with growing popular cynicism and lack of trust in institutions, Canadian foundations, most of which are governed and led by white people, some of whom may be members of families that have benefited from a capitalist economy that has its origins in colonialism, are accused of not doing enough to "check their privilege." Foundations can certainly be criticized for their risk aversion and their reluctance to act more directly either as advocates or as funders of social movements focused on changing systems. Neutral or evidence-based solutions to problems of inequality won't be enough. As David Callahan, an influential observer of American philanthropy noted in 2018, "Many foundations seem trapped in a dated mindset about how change happens and how to have impact. They haven't wrapped their heads around key realities of our age, like the fall of public trust in institutions and elites, and rising polarization and populism. In this environment, expertise just doesn't seem to matter all that much. What's moving change right now are social movements, ideology, and tribal loyalties."[14]

I argue in this book that the foundation world is not as unmoving as Callahan suggests. In 2021 we are seeing significant changes in the practice of charitable giving in Canada and elsewhere. Philanthropy is being transformed by the digital world, as is every sector in our society. The implications of these changes are only dimly seen. Will the familiar foundation structure of a perpetual self-governed (and government-regulated) endowment, which has remained remarkably unchanged in over a century, be transformed, or even disappear? We don't know enough yet. The ways in which private philanthropy acts for public benefit may indeed shift away from a foundation form and into social enterprises, non-profit think tanks and institutes, and digital platforms with fewer regulations and restrictions than the traditional charitable foundation model. What will this mean for philanthropic accountability and transparency? The foundations I write about are asking themselves these questions and are making the shifts that predict a more significant transformation. They may be few, but their examples and decisions are influential. Their actions will have an impact on the wider fields of philanthropy and civil society, and so it is important we understand them better.

The consequences of the COVID-19 pandemic are already profound, and no less so for private philanthropy. This book is not focused on the philanthropic response to the pandemic, but there are early indications of substantial movement in the practices of Canadian private foundations as they have responded to the crisis. Foundations face widespread non-profit sector restructuring and a need to rethink their own practices. We have witnessed a remarkably rapid shift in the short term to more flexible granting, more general operating support, and new commitments to grantees. Will this be an enduring shift toward more trust-based and more empowering grantmaking? It is difficult to see a complete recoil to past practice. My purpose is to show that this movement was already taking place before the crisis made it more obvious. The individual foundation stories that follow are a snapshot in time of a period in which the pace of change is finally beginning to accelerate.

The Landscape of Private Foundations in Canada

In this chapter, I step back to look at the foundation landscape more broadly before turning to the illustration of specific themes and approaches being used by the individual Canadian foundations I have chosen to profile. It's fair to say the world of private foundations in Canada remains largely unknown. Dr Susan Phillips, a leading academic researcher of philanthropy in Canada, has described private foundations as "akin to giraffes: ethereal, aristocratic and slow-moving creatures that should not exist, but they do, surrounded by a certain mystique."[1] While the description seems far-fetched, there are some reasons for this mystique. The private foundation sector is relatively new in historical terms. Most Canadian private foundations have existed in their current form only since the middle of the twentieth century. Until after the end of the Second World War, the charitable sector in Canada was supported mainly by religious organizations and private donors. While a few private trusts and foundations were created in the early part of the twentieth century, mainly to support the development of new civic institutions on a local or national level, the growth in numbers and size of private foundations only began to accelerate in the latter part of the century.

Another reason for this mystique is that many, if not most, of the private foundations in Canada are vehicles for individual or family philanthropy and the donors choose to keep their philanthropy low profile. The low profile is more common to private foundations run by families. Most private foundations are very small and operate as extensions of the family's personal giving, which the donors want to do privately or to be known only to their gift recipients. These private foundation creators are not invested in communicating about what they consider to be their personal choices. It is true that some multimillion-dollar gifts by private foundations are well publicized, usually by the recipients and usually to thank the donor and draw attention to the work of the receiving organization at the same time. But most families are happier to remain quiet givers.

The use of the term "private" is somewhat misleading. It is used by the federal government, which differentiates, for regulatory purposes, between foundations controlled by a single donor or set of related donors, classified as "private," and those not under the control of any single group, classified as "public." Not all so-called private foundations are family foundations. Some are foundations that might have started with the gift of a donor family but are no longer directed by the original donor or family and are now "independent." Corporate foundations also fall into the private category because their funds come from a single donor (the corporation). Independent and corporate foundations, although they fall into the government's category of "private," tend to be more visible than family foundations; more of them maintain websites and post public information about their goals and activities. Among the most prominent corporate foundations in Canada are those connected to the financial sector, such as the RBC Foundation, or the PriceWaterhouseCoopers Canada Foundation, and the energy sector, such as the Suncor Energy Foundation. These foundations share, through their branding and personnel, an association with the community and corporate affairs of their parent. The "public" foundations, like corporate private foundations, make themselves visible for deliberate reasons. Many are fundraising community foundations, based in large and small communities across Canada. Other public foundations are donor-advised foundations that seek to make themselves known to potential new donors; examples are MakeWay or the TD Private Giving Foundation. These foundations invest in communications and media campaigns to draw attention to the expertise and opportunities they offer. Finally, many public foundations are parallel foundations connected to a linked charity for which they fundraise. For example, SickKids Foundation is one of the largest and best-known hospital foundations in Canada.

There are few public and accessible directories or catalogues of these foundations. This also contributes to lower public awareness. The major source of data on private foundations is the federal government, which maintains a database as the regulator of charities. The federal government began registering charities in 1967 and created the separate categories of private and public foundations in 1976. A private foundation is designated at the time of registration by the Charities Directorate of the Canada Revenue Agency (CRA).[2] The CRA offers a comprehensive open database on all registered charities. All foundations and charities must provide a detailed annual report and almost all the data in this report is made public through an online CRA listing of charities.[3] The grants made by every private foundation, including amounts and recipients, are posted in this open database. Because the data is open, it can be accessed and integrated into other platforms and searchable guides offered by non-profit or for-profit suppliers. Private foundations are visible in this way to anyone searching the CRA lists, even if they have not made individual efforts to become visible.

Private Foundations: A Portrait by the Numbers

What does the data from the federal government tell us about private foundations in Canada? Since 2000, there has been a significant increase in the registration of private foundations, which is driven by growth in the wealth held, inherited, or created by individuals, families, and corporations and by the expansion of tax incentives for giving introduced by the federal government particularly since 1997. The registration numbers from CRA suggest that the total number of public and private foundations has increased rapidly in the last fifteen years, even allowing for the downturn created by the financial crisis of 2007–08. In comparative terms, the number of registered private foundations has increased at a much faster rate than the number of public foundations (see Figure 1.1). In 2021, there were just over six thousand private foundations, compared to just under five thousand public foundations. In 2005, the number of registered private foundations was lower than that of public foundations, but growing wealth, new tax incentives for donors that made it possible to donate assets such as equities, and an increased interest in philanthropy have all contributed to the rapid rise of private foundations. Private foundations constitute approximately 7 per cent of the approximately eighty-six thousand registered charities in Canada. The geographic distribution of private foundations is skewed toward the eastern part of the country for historical and demographic reasons. Two-thirds of private foundations are found in Ontario and Quebec. The oldest foundations are found in Quebec, where wealthy business owners in Montreal created charitable trusts in the 1930s and 1940s. Over time, as the population and wealth of Ontario has increased, a larger number of foundations has been created in that province. Now almost half of the total number of registered private foundations are based in Ontario, and, more specifically, in the Greater Toronto Metropolitan Area.

There are few giants in the Canadian foundation landscape. Like a shallow pyramid with an extremely wide base, the Canadian private foundation sector includes many small, private foundations with endowments generally under $5 million. At the apex of the pyramid are a very small number of large foundations. The top 150 private foundations in 2018 included a handful with assets over $500 million. They rapidly decrease in size, down to about $40 million in assets. The remaining six thousand private foundations are all at or under $40 million.[4] This distribution of foundations by size is comparable to that found in the United States. But the sheer number of American foundations and their wealth means we see more billionaire American foundations and they are correspondingly much more visible.

In 2018, Canadian private foundations collectively held approximately $56.3 billion in assets and gave $2.6 billion in gifts to charities.[5] This picture is somewhat skewed by the presence in Canada of one extremely large private foundation, the Mastercard Foundation, an independent foundation with assets of $23.7 billion in 2018. This rapidly growing asset base makes the Mastercard Foundation one of the largest private foundations in the world, and far beyond the Canadian norm. The next two largest private foundations in Canada hold assets of around $2 billion each, significantly less than the Mastercard Foundation. Excluding Mastercard, the top 149 grantmaking foundations (by assets) in the country collectively held about $20.75 billion, or about 64 per cent of the assets held by all private foundations.[6] Similarly, the top 149 grantmaking foundations (excluding Mastercard) gave $1.34 billion in grants, or about 50 per cent of all grants made by private foundations. Relatively speaking, the assets and grants of the private foundation sector in Canada are very small compared to the expenditures of the public sector, or governments at all levels.

Private foundations in Canada typically have few or no staff, relying on family volunteers or family offices for their day-to-day management and

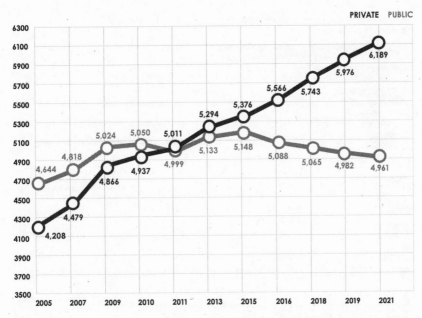

Fig. 1.1   Growth in numbers of private and public foundations 2005–21

outsourcing their financial services and reporting. The presence of paid staff is related, in many cases, to the nature of the foundation activities. The larger private foundations will usually have staff to manage their grants. They may also have staff to manage their own activities and programs, including conference and event convening, awarding of scholarships and prizes, publications, evaluation and impact measurement, policy development, and other activities that accompany grants management. But a considerable number of the large, private foundations still work with what could be called a skeleton staff of four or five full-time employees. Despite their assets, these foundations operate with little administrative overhead. The typical small family foundation may have a board of two or three unpaid directors, all of whom could be family members. Larger foundations would generally have between seven and nine directors, with a mix of family and non-family. There is no regulation that limits numbers or participation of family members. In practice, the number of family members on a family foundation board is decided by choice, interests, and availability.

Although the CRA database provides much so-called "tombstone" information, it does have some gaps. It does not tell us anything about the

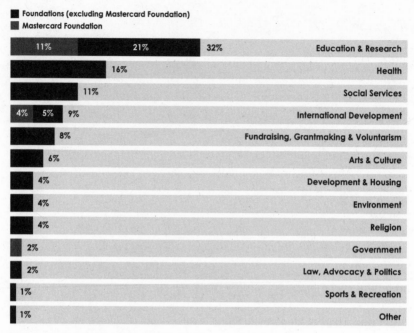

Fig. 1.2   Distribution of grants by activity area (%), 2018

diversity of private foundation donors or boards. We know little about the demographics of the families, boards, or staff of private foundations. There is also limited comparable public information on the fields of funding of Canadian foundations. The CRA data set tells us the names of individual foundation grantees and grant dollar amounts.[7] Based on this, we might think education and research is the single largest area of funding interest, measured by dollar amounts. In practice, we can see foundations give many grants, some of them substantial, to universities and colleges across Canada every year. However, the purposes of these grants can only be found in the information provided by the foundations and their grantees on an individual basis. Not all grants classified as "education" will be to improve education. After education and research, the largest amounts of philanthropic dollars go to health institutions and social services organizations. Together, education and research (32 per cent of grant dollars), health (16 per cent), and social services (11 per cent) received almost half of grant dollars in 2018 as shown in Figure 1.2. This pattern appears consistent year over year. And it is comparable to the pattern found in the United States, where health, education, and human services are ranked first, second, and third in terms of grant dollars awarded.[8]

What Is Driving the Growth of Private Foundations?

The Canadian private foundation sector is clearly expanding, and this expansion has been evident for at least two decades. The growing wealth of the country is one factor. Others are changes in demographics, population diversity, and a developing infrastructure of support organizations and advisers.

The large baby boom generation (born 1950–61) is retiring. As of July 2021, 18.5 per cent of the Canadian population was sixty-five or older.[9] More than one in two older persons are from the baby boom. As this generation ages and retires, it is considering what to do with the wealth it has either inherited or generated. Estimates[10] suggest that close to $1 trillion will be inherited in the next decade. At least some of this inheritance will go to philanthropy. Baby boom grandparents, who are eager to pass on a family legacy or looking for ways to engage with their younger family members, may well turn to a family foundation vehicle for this purpose.

From the point of view of the even larger millennial generation (born 1980–94), which is about 27 per cent of the Canadian population,[11] the opportunity for some of these children and grandchildren of the baby boomers to engage in work with social purpose is shifting the field. Creators of private foundations who come from earlier generations may approach philanthropy more conservatively. Members of Canada' sizeable millennial generation are now well into their working lives. For them, philanthropy is a chance to have impact on the complex problems that face the world, including growing inequality and increasingly dire environmental and climate change. Private foundations, particularly those governed by families, can offer young people an opportunity to engage in philanthropy at relatively early periods in their lives, and to do so with very different approaches from those of their parents or grandparents. Some young people are taking on part- or full-time leadership positions in their family foundations and approaching their philanthropy from a more synthetic perspective, looking at their resources as both financial and human, and engaging explicitly in social change not only as funders but as convenors and builders of capacity, and not only with charities but with non-profits, social enterprises, and businesses. A good example of this approach is the Daymark Foundation launched in 2021 and led by younger millennial members of the Michael McCain family with the bold intention of having a transformative impact, with its partners, on mental health in Canada. Other examples are the Northpine and Thistledown foundations, created by couples who are partners and beneficiaries of technology company growth and led by millennials committed to thoughtful and strategic philanthropic investments in combatting the effects of climate change and supporting vulnerable communities.

Canada also has a much more diverse and more urbanized population than it did fifty years ago. How does this potentially affect private philanthropy? It brings fresh players and new money to the table and new practitioners to the field. Many of Canada's immigrants start family businesses, and some of these are now operating in global markets. The Saputo Company of Montreal is an example of a family business created by Lino Saputo in the mid-1950s that is now a global corporation. This corporate success enabled the Saputo family to create a private foundation in 1980 that holds over $490 million in assets (in 2020). Philanthropic foundations started by more recent immigrants may also foster an interest in addressing global challenges, such as refugee and migrant settlement, and racism and social inclusion. Or they bring ideas about entrepreneurship and social innovation to the table because they are shaped by the experience of starting something new. An example of the latter would be the Trico Foundation of Calgary, created by Wayne and Eleanor Chiu in 2008. The Chius built a successful housing development business after moving to Canada in 1982. The Trico Foundation, named after the first letters of the five corporate values of the Chius' business, is focused on building social entrepreneurship, which emerged from the Chius' own passion for entrepreneurship and their awareness of the need for creative solutions to ensuring sustainability in the non-profit sector. Another example is the Bhayana Family Foundation of Toronto, a private foundation created in 2007 by the Bhayana family from the South Asian community with a unique focus on recognition of the people who work in the non-profit sector. Raksha Bhayana has led a decade-long philanthropic funding effort to celebrate, with awards and public ceremonies, the contributions and impact of professionals working in the non-profit sector. Through partnerships with United Ways across the country, and through successful advocacy campaigns to persuade governments and politicians to recognise and appreciate the sector, she and the Bhayana Foundation are building public awareness and creating conditions for more systematic public investment in the sector.

While information on philanthropic giving by newer immigrants in Canada is not easily available, it seems likely that as wealth grows in these communities, philanthropy also grows. We know that diaspora or cross-border giving by these communities is significant although we have very limited data on the dimensions of this giving. Within Canada itself, one of the leading experts on immigrant and diaspora giving, Krishan Mehta, suggests that "The role of immigrant communities in civic life and philanthropy has the potential to become one of Canada's enduring symbols, especially since concepts of giving are imbedded in so many different cultural practices. In other words, philanthropy is not only a marker of citizenship but also a unifying force that binds together people of diverse backgrounds."[12] The Judaic and Islamic traditions of *tzedakah*, *zakat*, and *sadaqah* have already played a powerful role in building significant philanthropic institutions, some of which are public like the Aga Khan Foundation Canada, strongly supported by the Ismaili community, or the Azrieli Foundation, which is a significant grantor to the Jewish community in Canada and in Israel. Many other foundations created by faith-driven donors remain private.

The role of women as donors and foundation decision-makers is another characteristic of private foundation philanthropy that has been evolving over time. While relatively few women have created private foundations on their own, as spouses and partners they can play prominent roles. We do not have specific data on the number of private foundations led exclusively by women, but we know that men and women sit together on the boards of many family foundations, and more private foundations are employing women as staff leads. According to research by Investor Economics and TD Wealth, women are likely to be the primary beneficiaries of the transfer of wealth over the next decade and, by the end of 2024, may control up to $3 trillion in personal financial wealth.[13] "The increase in the total income generated by women, as well as the likelihood that they will be substantial inheritors over the next decade, suggests that women can and will play an increasingly powerful role in Canadian philanthropy."[14] Research would also indicate that women tend to give more to causes related to poverty, health, children, education, and women's rights, linking their values to their charitable goals and desired impact.[15] To the extent that their giving is structured through a private foundation, we may see a shift over the next few years in the cause areas where private foundations are most active. The different track record of newly independent women philanthropists in the United States, such as Melinda French Gates and Mackenzie Scott, suggests women might be willing to make bold decisions in making grants that have fewer restrictions and that are left to recipients to spend as they need, rather than as what the donor thinks is important. We don't yet have such examples in Canada, but it is likely we will see them in the next decade.

In the Indigenous communities of Canada, while there is strong demographic growth, and some increasing ownership of resources, there are few structured foundations. Using a model that is closer to Indigenous philanthropic traditions, we are beginning to see the growth of more community foundations and collaborative funds focused on mutual pooling of funds and shared resources. In a later chapter I discuss how non-Indigenous private foundations are beginning to work more closely with Indigenous communities to build relationships and exchanges.

The Professionalization of the Foundation Sector

What else has contributed to the growth of private foundations? Over the last three decades, the Canadian private foundation sector has been given further structure and depth through the creation of infrastructure organizations and more collaborative activities. Foundation boards and staff have had more opportunities for professionalization through education and attention by consultants and academic researchers. These developments have contributed to greater awareness and interest in creating a private foundation vehicle.

Two umbrella organizations have supported the growth of an enabling environment for private philanthropy: the Centre for Canadian Philanthropy (now Imagine Canada), and Philanthropic Foundations Canada (PFC), a dedicated network for private foundations that has evolved into a network bringing together various philanthropic foundations, both private and public. For two decades, PFC, the network I led until 2019, has been collecting and publicizing stories about the work of private foundations to create a sense of the possibilities of private philanthropy, and to inspire an interest among donors in creating a foundation.

The academic world is also beginning to recognize foundations as a field of study in Canada. Initially focused more on philanthropy from a recipient-charity perspective, universities in Canada offered centres of study and certification for professionals in fundraising or education for donors. In Ontario in 2013, Carleton University launched the first graduate-level professional training program with its masters and diploma in Philanthropy and Nonprofit Leadership, and it explicitly included foundation leaders and staff as possible student recruits. The same year, the Montreal Laboratory for Research on Canadian Philanthropy (PhiLab) began its work at the Université du Québec à Montréal, specializing in studies of private and public grantmaking foundations, particularly their work on systemic efforts to address inequalities due to poverty and environmental change. These academic centres, and the faculty and students associated with them, are developing research papers and studies that are increasing the awareness and understanding of the impact of grantmaking foundations.

The field of philanthropic advising has grown in the last two decades and this has turned the attention of more donors to the potential of private foundation work. Family offices and financial advisers have more information, more tools, and more incentives to steer their clients toward establishing private foundations. While the field of financial advising still may be oriented more to estate planning for clients than to the promise and personal fulfilment of engaging in philanthropic work, research[16] conducted by the Canadian Association of Gift Planners and others is building a business case for financial advisers and family office managers to hold informed "philanthropic conversations" on an ongoing basis with their clients. Advisers agree that the ability to engage in a client conversation that goes beyond tax and legal advice to explore the personal motives and opportunities for private philanthropy will deepen client relationships. Their advice is likely to be contributing in some degree to the increase we are seeing in the numbers of registrations of private foundations.

Private Philanthropy:
Lifespan, Role, and Independence

In my view, three characteristics of private foundations are particularly important to their identity and contribute to their appeal to donors: long life, a primary role as funder of other charities, and independence. Of these three, neither lifespan nor grantmaking are the *most* valuable elements of a private foundation identity. Independence in thought, means, and action may be the most important aspect of a foundation's role. To understand this, it is worth looking at each of these three foundation characteristics in turn.

THE LIFESPAN OF THE PRIVATE FOUNDATION

One of the questions faced by private foundation creators is the lifespan of their philanthropic vehicle. How long should a private foundation exist? This is an ongoing public debate, which engages both critics and proponents of private foundations. Many assume private foundations are always set up as endowments to endure in perpetuity, or into an indefinite future with no limit. But there is no legal requirement in Canada that private foundations be set up as perpetual endowments. Foundations can be set up as charitable trusts or they can be constituted as not-for-profit corporations. In either situation, as charities, they are not required to wind down at a specific time. Their donors may make provision through a direction to the trustees or directors that the foundation operate for the long term through prudent stewardship of the funds. The donor may specify that they wish the foundation to spend only the interest on its invested capital and not the capital itself. But the donor could remain silent on this question or give flexibility to the trustees or directors of the foundation to encroach on the capital if needed. A private foundation can even be funded and disbursed on an annual basis, without endowment, although this is less common.

An explicit decision on lifespan is linked to the intent, vision, or motivation of the donor, and to the idea of legacy. In the absence of an explicit intent, the default position is an indefinite organizational time horizon, which can be described as perpetuity. Many, if not most, private foundations would perceive themselves as "long-life" foundations, particularly if more than one generation of a founding family is involved. How long is long? It could be a generation, or beyond a generation; it could be much shorter. In the American private foundation sector, there are private foundations that are famously tied to the lifespans of their founders, such as the Gates Foundation. Some foundations choose a "spend-down" strategy, such as the Andrea and Charles Bronfman Philanthropies or the Atlantic Philanthropies, both of which wound down after existing for between thirty and forty years. These so-called limited-life foundations are still in a minority, with numbers variously estimated at between 10 per cent and 25 per cent of private foundations in the United States.[17] While there is no data on the numbers of private foundations in Canada that have explicitly chosen a spend-down approach, it is reasonable to assume the proportion would be similar. The limited-life model also tends to be favoured by younger philanthropists who have made fortunes in the technology or financial services sector, or by other engaged donors who want to see the impact of their philanthropic dollars in their lifetimes, or to "give while they live." Such donors are less motivated by an interest in leaving a family legacy vehicle for their second and subsequent generations. Even though most private foundations appear to have chosen a longer organizational lifespan, this is not a predetermining or defining characteristic. The choice of lifespan is more strongly connected to how the foundation chooses to do its work. And this is a choice each foundation makes independently. This brings us to the second assumed characteristic of private foundations: their role as grantmakers.

PRIVATE FOUNDATIONS AS GRANTMAKERS

Across countries where private foundations have been a favoured structure for philanthropic giving over the past century, such as the United States, Canada, and the United Kingdom, the primary role of such foundations has been understood to be that of grantmaker, or provider of monetary resources to other charities. When foundations are first established, that may well be the case. But the role can change over time. New generations, changing missions, and internal developments in the foundation can alter the nature of the foundation's activities. Indeed, a private foundation in Canada has no regulatory obligation to make grants at all if its stated purpose does not commit it to doing so. It can devote all its resources to its own programs, much as an operating charity does. Or it could pursue a mix of grantmaking and operational activities. The role of arms-length grantmaker does not have to be central to the private foundation identity, even if it is so in the popular mind.

Private foundations in Canada play many different roles. Through the power of their financial resources and their independence of choice, they can play the role of grantor or investor. They can also act as convenors, network builders, influencers, and advocates. A scholar of Australian foundations captures the variety of the roles played by private foundations in another way, through their actions: "[They] mediate, intercede, intervene, arrange, broker, buffer and filter."[18] The brokering, buffering, and filtering roles are common to family foundations that act as grantmaking intermediaries between their donors and the charities to which they make grants. The mediation, intervention, and arranging roles played by a smaller number of private foundations take them into more substantial operating mode, often with the need to manage staff, researchers, partners, and peers. As with the choice of lifespan, the choice of roles is very much connected to a foundation's mission and how it chooses to work toward it, in other words its choice of strategy. This choice is what transforms the foundation's role from straightforward grantmaker into a more complex set of functions, whether managing its own activities as a program manager and/or social investor, or in roles that involve funding and participating in activities such as training, publications, meetings, and consulting.

PRIVATE FOUNDATIONS AS INDEPENDENT AGENTS

A third and critical characteristic of private foundations is their independence – of thought, means, and operations. This does not mean they are free to act in any way they see fit. Regulatory guardrails maintained by the federal government in Canada ensure charitable funds are being held and disbursed for charitable purposes. All Canadian charities must disburse an annual minimum percentage of invested assets on charitable activities. In addition, for private foundations, there are provisions against self-dealing in the *Income Tax Act*. These provisions are there to prevent the kind of activity that, in theory, could be undertaken by a foundation controlled by a single individual or set of related individuals who decide to use the assets of the foundation for private, and not for public, benefit. In practice, there are very few instances of private foundations in Canada having their registration revoked for self-dealing.

This independence in service of the public is highly valued by foundation donors and by their boards, and they apply it to their choices of what and whom to fund, as well as for how long. As noted, a private foundation is free to make an independent decision about the temporal nature of its work, which is a question it could ask itself at various points in its history. McGeorge Bundy, the president of the Ford Foundation in the 1960s and '70s, noted in 1966 that "a foundation should regularly ask itself if it could do more good dead than alive," but went on to conclude that "we find that there is no present reason to believe that the world will have less need of a large foundation in 1980 than in 1967; the forces we help to counterbalance are not likely to be smaller – the need for an independent agency not likely to be less."[19] This thought captures both the nature of a private foundation's ability to decide on its institutional longevity and also the value of being an independent player in balancing the forces that act negatively on society.

Defenders of private foundations in North America and Europe have generally cited the independence of private foundations as one of their key attributes. In the United Kingdom, where there is no mandated government payout rule for endowed foundations, the Association of Charitable Foundations has argued that "the independence of charitable foundations ... is part of what makes them an enduring and irreplaceable asset within civil society. Their financial independence supports research, enables a plurality of voices that can inform public debates, and backs 'unpopular' causes or places where the need is great. Unlike most other types of funder, their independence allows them to take a long view free from short-term political or economic cycles, and to respond creatively to immediate need as well as take a long-term approach."[20] Joel Fleishman, an academic historian of American philanthropy, has been even more unequivocal in his defense of the autonomy of foundations: "I believe that the dynamism, robustness, diversity, and rich texture of the American civic sector depends on the continuing freedom of American foundations to deploy their charitable resources to any causes they may choose, free of intimidation and coercion by anyone, especially government."[21] In a 2004 speech, one of the leaders of Canadian private philanthropy, Tim Brodhead, the former president of the McConnell Foundation, put the case less aggressively but no less strongly: "The 'value proposition' philanthropy offers is about the private satisfaction of the donor and meeting important social needs. In a world of polarities – good/bad, right/wrong, rich/poor, mine/yours – philanthropy creates a bridge. It links private and public – personal commitment, individual initiative, private wealth and the public good, collective responsibility, community well-being. It says, 'We are not islands; we can choose, freely, to act for the common good.'"[22] This reflection connects the value of independent agency and choice to the role foundations play as funders of local and national communities.

Private foundations can create unique and enduring social value. The mysterious and slow-moving giraffes of the private foundation field captured in Dr Phillips' vivid metaphor are certainly still there. But, in my view, far from being giraffes, some private foundations are more like dolphins: intelligent, purposeful, curious, flexible, willing to work together. Dolphins, like human beings, are aware of the power of communication, and can work together in pursuit of a long-term goal.

While it may be difficult to picture a private foundation in the same universe as that of a swift and intelligent marine mammal, it is possible to find examples in the Canadian landscape today of such philanthropic creatures. They are not in the majority, but they are growing in number. I tell the stories of these dolphin-like philanthropies in this book. To set the stage for individual stories, I take a closer look in the next chapter at the wider organizational changes and evolution of approaches to foundation strategy.

The Changing Roles of Foundations

Good granting is both an art and a science. It takes the heart to understand and to discern what is true and the head to ensure rigour and effectiveness.

Tim Brodhead

Private foundations in Canada, as in Europe, the United Kingdom, and the United States, have an almost unlimited liberty to choose where and how they will make their difference to society. The philanthropic foundation form is common to many countries even if there is no uniform legal definition. In each of these societies, foundations governed by private citizens make decisions that have important social, policy, and sometimes political impact over time. Yet, in most cases, we do not know much about how they make their decisions, and how they go about the task of defining their goals and selecting their tools to achieve their purposes. As more of these foundations begin to explain their choices to the public, we are starting to understand more about the pressures and opportunities to which these foundations are responding.

Over the last two decades, I have seen many philanthropic foundations evolve as they work on a social change agenda, moving beyond their initial role as personal philanthropy vehicles for donors. These foundations are experimenting with proactive strategies that range from designing and funding their own projects and partners, to engaging in more convening and collaborative work with peers. They are not relying exclusively on a traditional and individualized approach to charitable funding. A few are starting to work in a participatory mode of philanthropy where community partners lead, and foundations follow. Why have these foundations come to think differently about their approaches? In most cases they have moved well beyond the role of an arms-length, disengaged maker of grants. How has this come about?

How Do Private Foundations Think About Strategy?

For many foundations, the first decision is to adopt a mission, coupled perhaps with strategic goals. The choice of goals starts with the question: "What social good do we want to do with the resources we have?" Creating a strategy involves making choices of what to do with finite resources. So, foundations must choose where to put their assets of money, people, and time. They must do some serious thinking about what matters to them, what skills they might have or need, and with whom they want to work. Phil Buchanan, leader of the US Center for Effective Philanthropy, and an adviser on what he calls "giving done right," breaks down the task of building a plan for philanthropic giving into four elements: "clear goals, coherent strategies, disciplined implementation, and good performance indicators."[1] But, he goes on to warn, doing it well is "uniquely challenging … it takes commitment, humility and a willingness to understand the nuance."

This is difficult work. Foundation boards and leaders must consider many issues if they want to put a philanthropic strategy into play. Internally, foundations need to organize themselves to use their capital effectively through the tools of investments, grants, and program budgets. They must identify the outcomes they might hope for, the indicators and feedback that would help them learn from their work, and the staff capacities they might need to get it done. Externally, they must manage relations with their grantees and partners, whether these are organizations receiving their support or external collaborators in the work, including other foundations. They must figure out how to act more transparently and demonstrate accountability to the community. And they must understand their place in the larger system that they are trying to change.

This question of place in a system is becoming more important to consider in the 2020s as social media and the publicity attracted by large philanthropic gifts draw more scrutiny to the strategies of foundations. They are making decisions in an environment that is changing rapidly. On the investment side, the assets being managed in foundation endowments are drawing critical attention. Foundations are being challenged to deploy more of their capital into investments with a social purpose or impact. It is no longer an unquestioned practice to separate investment policy from mission, as private foundations have done in the past, and to ignore the social impact of these investments. On the granting side, foundations are coming under pressure from communities to provide more unrestricted, multi-year, or general operating support, or to involve their partners directly in their decision-making about grants. This pressure was beginning to build before 2019 but has been intensified by the impact of the pandemic. Many of the organizations foundations work with are inherently fragile and under-resourced. Foundations are being asked to consider whether their own processes and requirements in providing funds might, in fact, be adding to, instead of reducing, this fragility. Foundations are being pushed to acknowledge the power differences between themselves and their grantees and partners, open their decision-making, and engage the views and voices of those who seek foundation resources with which to do their work. To be fair, the pressure to ask these questions is not just external. Foundation staff and board members themselves are proactively raising them, and probably arguing about how to answer them.

In the face of these external pressures and internal questions, more foundations are becoming attuned to the context in which they do their work. They exist in an ecosystem of funders and partners, not simply as individual grantmakers working in isolation with their grantees. As foundations become more intentional about their strategies, the importance of being aware of the landscape and operating context increases correspondingly. This also implies a greater need for open communication about how and why they choose to use their resources in the community, particularly if they are intent on supporting social change. Canadian private foundations have been slow in the past to react to the pressure for sharing information about themselves and their strategies. In a 2016 assessment of the largest family foundations in Canada (measured by size of endowments), Dr Susan Phillips of Carleton University noted that "the majority of foundations do not publicly communicate a strategy or strong rationale for why they support what they do, and in coming years can expect to be under increased scrutiny as to where the money goes."[2] She based this statement on a review of these foundations' public communications, including whether or not they had a website. Many did not.

No doubt the effort to articulate and communicate philanthropic strategy is demanding, and the resources to do it are few, especially for smaller foundations. Yet asset size doesn't correspond to an articulated strategy nor more frequent or open communication. Even if it appears logical that the more resources you have as a foundation, the more you are likely to think about strategy and to communicate your goals, asset size is not a good predictor of engagement in strategic philanthropy. It isn't resources alone that drive proactive communication or planning. Small and large foundations choose the more familiar approach, which is one of responding to funding requests without, as Phil Buchanan puts it, "a logic to guide decisions to achieve goals."[3] With this approach, the communication of a strategy is next to impossible. The silence from many foundations that act primarily as responsive funders is one of the reasons the Canadian foundation sector has seemed so opaque, and why so little still is known about the actions of foundations. It is why Dr Phillips has described private foundations as mysterious creatures. Yet, having said this, Phillips also recognizes that more proactive foundations are important actors in the broader social and economic landscape of Canada today. She points out that their role can go far beyond that of charitable funder. "The distinctive position of philanthropic foundations in an unfolding reconfiguration of relationships among the public, private and non-profit sectors ... is as important as their financial capacity. Private foundations have a comparative advantage in being able to align with or mediate among non-profits, businesses, and governments. Their discretionary, patient capital, can provide the unrestricted, or highly targeted, financing that mobilizes other players and supports social innovation. Private foundations can shape public discourses and influence or co-create policy agendas," and, she concludes, this would be done "ideally in a transparent manner."[4] The more a foundation is active in this way, the more it is also taking on the obligation to disclose and communicate to the public its goals and strategies.

Is Philanthropic Strategy Like Business Strategy?

A growing group of Canadian private foundations over the last two decades has chosen to become more focused and intentional. In most cases, these foundations pursue a mix of strategies; the mix varies from foundation to foundation and even within a single foundation over time. It's not the strategies themselves that they hold in common but more that they pursue a proactive determination to work toward defined goals. This does not mean they are adopting the "philanthrocapitalism" approach I referred to in the opening chapter. Admittedly, as Ben Soskis, an American historian of philanthropy, has put it, this business-like approach to philanthropy is "perhaps the most dominant mode of thinking about philanthropy in the

2000s ... drawing sustenance from the much deeper narrative reservoir of the epic hero. ... A bold leader takes on a clearly defined problem, poses a well-defined solution, and assumes great risks, resulting in a clear resolution: either victory or failure."[5] It is a particularly appealing approach for the wealthy entrepreneurial donors who have been successful in business; they tend to create foundations as philanthropic vehicles for action on social issues, employing targeted, top-down strategies.

Philanthrocapitalism as a strategic approach has been somewhat tarnished by its association with the American technology or financial market billionaires who have used business models and metrics to try to "fix" social challenges, such as poverty or lack of access to education, and have not had the success they expected. In Canada, in the early 2000s, we had far fewer of these entrepreneurial billionaires, and far fewer large foundations. This is not to conclude that we have no exponents of a business-like approach to philanthropy. But in general, Canadian philanthropy has followed a more cautious approach to the application of business thinking to social problems and business metrics to the determination of social impact.

Does this mean that the group of foundations whose stories I tell in the following pages do not pursue a "strategic" approach? Not at all. If strategy is defined by an intentional approach to the allocation of resources to achieve a social purpose, then all these foundations can be described as strategic. Yet it is important to add a nuance to this term. Canada is certainly influenced by some of the models and debates on foundation strategies that we have witnessed in the much larger philanthropic foundation sector in the United States. Since 1999, an argument has raged in the United States about so-called "strategic philanthropy," an approach defined by "clear goals, data-driven strategies, heightened accountability, and rigorous evaluations."[6] This approach, described by Michael Porter and Mark Kramer in an influential 1999 *Harvard Business Review* article,[7] proposed that foundations can best create value for society by "focusing on a clear and limited set of goals, conducting thorough research, framing a hypothesis for how best to approach the problem, and developing an evidence-based process for learning from results."[8] Many foundations in the United States, and some in Canada, worked to develop logic models and theories of change to explain (at least to themselves) the work they were doing and the results or outcomes they hoped to achieve. After fifteen years of experience, and some failures, thinking about strategic philanthropy has become less linear. Some of the same consultants, such as Mark Kramer, who proposed the idea of strategic philanthropy, acknowledged that it wasn't always possible to be clear about how foundation actions could drive to specific outcomes, and suggested that they had not considered the differences between simple, complicated, and complex social problems.[9] Complexity is a characteristic of many social problems, with intersectional elements in many cases. To take an example, poor school performance in certain neighbourhoods can be linked to lack of early childhood development, poor housing and transportation, inadequate family support, language barriers, and systemic racism, to name just a few factors. What do you work on first to fix school performance and how do you determine the optimal use of your limited resources? As Phil Buchanan has observed, "Strategy in philanthropy isn't easy even in the best circumstances in terms of available evidence because even when something seems like it would make sense, even when there's evidence that it might work or does work, that doesn't always mean it will work in practice or in every context."[10] This suggests that foundation strategy needs to be more evolving than fixed, more flexible than well-defined, more about testing and learning than prescribing and evaluating. Philanthropic funders may begin with a fixed idea and plan, but evolve with feedback, and experience. Most of the foundations I discuss in this book have followed this path. They practise what Phil Buchanan calls "total strategy," focusing on what works, gathering evidence, and shifting when necessary. They are also willing to collaborate with partners, and to know when they don't know. This is not business strategy but philanthropy strategy, not exclusive but inclusive, not fixed but emergent, not prescriptive but responsive to changing conditions.

It would be going too far to conclude that philanthropic strategy is not at all like strategy in a business context. While collaboration may be more normal for philanthropy than competition, and there is no patent on philanthropic "products," there are, or ought to be, some commonalities with business organizations. Just as businesses need to focus on their customers, so do foundations and charities need to be alert to clients and audiences. Both for-profit and non-profit organizations can benefit from gathering and analyzing relevant information. Scanning the landscape, seeking feedback from customers or clients (or grantees in the case of foundations), and applying learning to adjust or innovate practice are equally important tools for businesses and foundations. But a crucial difference in philanthropic strategy is the mindset. In business, the mindset is one of control and competition. In philanthropy, the mindset must be one of humility and collaboration. Phil Buchanan is a careful analyst and sharp critic of the overused comparison of business to philanthropy, and he draws a firm distinction between business and philanthropic approaches to strategy. He confirms that strategy in both cases requires a decision-making logic, goal setting, evidence, and measurement of progress. But, as he observes, "absent a competitive context, strategy plays out differently [for philanthropy]. It's not about the giver having all the control. It's about a collection of different actors working together and responding to continual feedback. Strategy is crucial in philanthropy, but it needs to be applied in a way that is mindful of the unique challenges of working on the most vexing, complicated and interdependent issues."[11] In this way, philanthropic strategy is very different than the strategies developed in the world of business.

Philanthropic Strategy: Discovery and the Long-term View

If a foundation has chosen to be strategic, to be proactive in reaching for goals, what tools or approaches might it pursue? The first approach is simply to make grants to organizations working toward the same goals. This approach is common to almost all the foundations I look at in this book. But it is far from the only one. Dr Phillips, in her 2018 study[12] of thirty-eight large family foundations in Canada, describes five categories of approaches private foundations can employ in their work, including grantmaking. While she discussed these approaches in a specific context as ways in which private philanthropy intersects with public management and policy, they are not unique to the sphere of philanthropy and public policy alone. They can be applied as approaches to the effort of making social change, whether it takes place through public policy development or fieldwork, through research or infrastructure building. Considering philanthropic strategy in this way, the focus shifts from the specific activity of a foundation, such as grantmaking, to the purpose of a foundation, which can be about trying to change a system, policy, or set of circumstances for the benefit of society.

The five approaches to philanthropic work described by Dr Phillips are: grantmaking, discovery, construction, illumination, and co-creation.

Grantmaking has a *distributive* function, a sharing of financial resources. Discovery has an *innovation* function, supporting early stages of a new approach to a social problem. Construction has a *field-building* function, lending support to the formation of networks and movements. Illumination has a *creative* function, stimulating the generation of ideas through research, discussion, and shaping of conceptual frameworks to solve problems. Co-creation has an *activist and advocacy* function, making social progress through public policy development, for example. Phillips's categories offer a deeper and more nuanced way to characterize the strategic approaches that are open to foundations with a changemaking purpose. This analysis helps us to understand that the redistribution of financial resources through grantmaking is far from the only way in which we could or should describe the work of such foundations.

Phillips's analysis opens a broader perspective on how private foundations can and even *should* act to make social change. This perspective is mirrored to some extent in the work of Robert Reich, a political philosopher at Stanford University, who discussed private foundation strategies in his 2018 book *Just Giving: Why Philanthropy Is Failing Democracy and How It Can Do Better*. Reich was interested in answering the question: What is the role of philanthropy, both individual and organized philanthropy, in a liberal democratic society? And what role *should* it play? He was pursuing the specific question of whether the public, through the state, should be willing not only to tolerate but also to encourage through tax incentives a form of private activity, philanthropy, that is not itself democratic. Like Phillips, Reich looks beyond grantmaking. Indeed, in his view, a strategic focus on pure redistributive strategies is not sufficient justification for public or state subsidy of private foundation resources. Reich makes his case for the existence of private foundations in a liberal democracy, but only if these foundations operate in roles that neither state nor market are likely to undertake, namely intergenerational justice and discovery. He argues that foundations are crucial organizations to counter the effects of "presentism," or "democracy's systematic and pervasive bias in favour of the present,"[13] which is one of its major liabilities. Because of their institutional design, foundations can use their resources to "fund higher risk social policy experiments and identify potential social problems decades away or innovations whose success might be apparent only after a longer time horizon."[14] In his view, foundations can and should do "what democratic governments routinely fail to do: think long."[15] He also points, like Phillips, to the importance of the discovery function, suggesting that it might be the most important one that a private foundation can serve. As he says, "Foundations, free of both marketplace or electoral accountability regimes, answerable to the diverse preferences and ideas of their donors, with an endowment designed to last decades or more, are especially well, perhaps uniquely, situated to engage in the sort of high-risk, long-run policy innovation and experimentation that is healthy in a democratic society and that addresses the interests of future generations."[16] He concludes that the state should provide encouragement to private philanthropy as long as it makes the important contribution of "taking an experimentalist long-time-horizon approach to policy innovation [and] to the project of promoting and securing justice across generations."[17] I have quoted Reich's thinking at length because it is an important reframing of the work of private foundations in ways that push beyond the seemingly straightforward but unidimensional description of "grantmaker."

Canadian Foundations as Partners in Social Change

How do we see these multiple roles playing out in the Canadian context? In the following pages, I describe the evolution of twenty Canadian foundations that, among them, represent the diversity of strategies in a philanthropic organization. While there are many foundations in Canada that have compelling stories, I applied somewhat arbitrary criteria for choosing and telling the stories of these foundations. They all have some combination of longevity, strategic goal setting, and commitment to sharing their work publicly that makes it possible to explore their work more fully, and to illustrate the valuable niche such foundations occupy in our social and economic ecosystem. Drawing on the categories described by Dr Phillips, I suggest that each of these grantmakers pursues one or more of the roles of discovery, construction, illumination, and co-creation.

While each foundation is different, it is possible to provide what could be called "tombstone" information about them for broad comparison purposes. Much of this information is summarized in Tables 2.1 and 2.2. These foundations range from among the oldest in the country to some of the newest. Most began as a vehicle created by individual donors to benefit community or create social good through their generosity. Most, though not all, hold and manage an invested endowment from which to fund their work. As Table 2.1 indicates, sixteen of them are in the top

Table 2.1   Summary of foundation data (2020)

Name	Year[1]	Assets[2]	Grants[3]	Number of Grants	Grants Range[4]	Program[5]	Board	Staff[6]
Azrieli (public)	1989	$2.28B	$68.0M	252	$2,500 to 7.0M	$22.9M	8	24
Chagnon (private)	2000	$2.15B	$17.0M	54	$5,000 to 8.6M	$46.3M	11	42
McConnell (private)	1967	$699.0M	$19.4M	381	$1,000 to 1.0M	$10.1M	15	45
Trottier (private)	2000	$235.7M	$18.6M	171	$5,000 to 2.9M	none	5	5
Metcalf (private)	1967	$181.0M	$6.4M	156	$2,500 to 535k	$1.4M	7	7
Donner (private)	1977	$155.0M	$4.0M	89	$5,000 to 385k	$971k	12	3
Lawson (private)	1967	$141.5M	$5.9M	177	$2,500 to 300k	$1.37M	11	7
Ivey (private)	1967	$109.4M	$3.85M	55	$5,000 to 250k	$919k	5	3
Atkinson (private)	1967	$100.4M	$2.7M	25	$6,000 to 678k	$1.5M	13	6
Hallman (public)	2003	$102.5M	$10.7M	57	$5,000 to 1.2M	$331k	6	3
Max Bell (private)	1967	$87.6M	$2.4M	46	$5,000 to 757k	none	4	4
Laidlaw (private)	1967	$81.9M	$3.2M	87	$2,000 to 535k	$2.26M	13	8
Gordon (private)	1967	$72.1M	$426k	34	$1,000 to 50k	$2.1M	15	13
Counselling (private)	1967	$58.6M	$2.9M	24	$2,500 to 1.2M	$825k	12	5
Catherine Donnelly (private)	2003	$50.9M	$1.2M	51	$5,000 to 50k	$1.7M	14	5
Inspirit (public)	1985	$42.0M	$1.1M	25	$2,500 to 113k	$620k	11	4
Muttart (private)	1967	$41.5M	$1.0M	74	$1,000 to 195k	$1.5M	7	6
Helderleigh (private)	2002	$17.3M	$1.5M	12	$5,000 to 407k	none	6	0
Boeckh (private)	1990	$7.7M	$32k	6	$1,575 to 14k	$2.5M	7	8
Maytree (private)	1982	$356k	$2.1M	27	$2,500 to 180k	$2.25M	8	13

Notes
1 Registration date with CRA (note that 1967 was first year that registration was required).
2 Assets: Total assets as of 31 December 2020 (Line 4200 T3010) and rounded up.
3 Total grants to qualified donees made in 2020 (Line 5050 T3010) and rounded up.
4 From smallest to largest in 2020.
5 Total amounts expended on charitable activities (excluding grants to qualified donees) (line 5000 T3010).
6 Permanent full-time as reported in Schedule 3 of T3010.

Source: All data reported in CRA T3010 database for year ending 2020-12-31
https://apps.cra-arc.gc.ca/ebci/hacc/srch/pub/dsplyBscSrch.

150 list of grantmaking foundations (ranked by invested assets). Two are very large with assets between $1 billion and $2 billion. The remainder hold invested assets ranging from over $600 million down to less than $35 million. The majority are in Montreal and the Greater Toronto Area; two are based in Alberta. In fifteen of the twenty, the original donor or family descendants are still engaged in the work of the foundation. Nine of them are led by women, and most have gender-balanced boards, although, as with many charities in Canada still, those boards lack diversity in other respects. Most of them have at least one, and in a few cases many, permanent staff members. Most or all are funders in the sense that they make grants to other charities, but they pursue their strategies through a mix of grants and contributions to programs of their partners and operating their own programs. They operate, in most cases, on a national scale, although many keep a strong connection to a local base. These foundations have experimented with strategies that range from defining their own projects and partners, to focusing on capacity-building and convening activity, to contributing to public policy development. They exemplify the discovery, construction, illumination, and co-creation functions described by Dr Phillips.

All the foundations I profile make regular and varied efforts to communicate their work through their own websites and, frequently, through additional reports, newsletters, blogs, and opinion pieces, as noted in Table 2.2. All of them see value in being members of the broader philanthropic community, and they engage actively in peer networks, such as PFC, Environment Funders Canada, and the Circle on Philanthropy and Aboriginal Peoples in Canada, as well as more focused funder groups and collaboratives. Their commitments to going beyond the

Table 2.2   Foundation use of communications (January 2022)

Name	Website	Annual/Biennial Report*	Publications/Newsletters/News Releases	Social Media
Azrieli (public)	✓		✓	
Chagnon (private)	✓		✓	
McConnell (private)	✓		✓	✓
Trottier (private)	✓		✓	✓
Metcalf (private)	✓	✓	✓	✓
Donner (private)	✓			
Lawson (private)	✓	✓	✓	✓
Ivey (private)	✓	✓	✓	
Atkinson (private)	✓		✓	✓
Hallman (public)	✓		✓	
Max Bell (private)	✓	✓	✓	
Laidlaw (private)	✓	✓	✓	✓
Gordon (private)	✓		✓	✓
Counselling (private)	✓	✓	✓	✓
Catherine Donnelly (private)	✓	✓	✓	✓
Muttart (private)	✓		✓	
Helderleigh (private)	✓		✓	
Boeckh (private)	✓		✓	✓
Maytree (private)	✓		✓	✓
Inspirit (public)	✓	✓	✓	✓

*   In addition to the annual report made to CRA

requirements for basic information reporting make it easier to understand and track the evolution of their strategies.

None of the foundations profiled in this book are corporate foundations, or foundations that are registered as private by the CRA, even though they are entities of public corporations. Corporate philanthropy is important in Canada, although there are not as many structured corporate foundations in Canada as there are in the United States, in relative terms. But I have not profiled any corporate foundations because I am interested in exploring foundations that have the combination of full strategic autonomy as well as a long-term horizon. The foundations I describe are similar in their internal structures. Yet regional and historical factors differentiate their strategies. For example, philanthropy in the two largest provinces, Quebec and Ontario, has somewhat different roots. Private philanthropy is a more recent phenomenon in francophone Quebec. There are more than twice as many private foundations in Ontario as in Quebec, even though Quebec is the second-largest province after Ontario and has the longest colonial history. Foundation work is taking place in a different cultural and political context in Quebec. According to Sylvain Lefèvre and Peter Elson, researchers affiliated with Montreal-based PhiLab, "the history of Quebec philanthropy has always been at variance with that of the rest of Canada. For example, in the decades following the Second World War, religion [the Catholic Church] played a central role in Quebec, while the welfare state was developing in the other provinces. ... Another long-lasting consequence of the Quiet Revolution, with repercussions on the decreasing role of foundations even today, was the institutionalization of strong relations between the government of Quebec and the community sector."[18] Long-term core funding of many civil society and community organizations by the Quebec government has meant a relatively smaller role played by private foundations in providing core funding to the community sector. Lefèvre and Elson comment that "when observing today's funding structure of community organizations in Quebec, we note the prominence of provincial funding, the very low level of federal funding, and the provision, even if this is a downward trend, of mission-based funding rather than service agreements or funding on a per-project basis. ... This funding configuration in Quebec helps to explain the unique contribution of the [Lucie et André] Chagnon Foundation."[19] This private foundation, one of the largest in Canada, operates exclusively in Quebec, and, for a decade, chose to fund a partnership directly with the Quebec government to support family and early child development in the province through three fully and jointly funded operating programs. This partnership wound up after a decade, and the Chagnon Foundation has publicly shared its reflections on the advantages and challenges of working so closely with government. Yet it is interesting to note it is not a model that has been repeated at this scale in any other Canadian jurisdiction. The state in Quebec is a critical and dominant actor in education, health, and social services, and for those

private foundations, both francophone and anglophone, that are based
in the province, public policy decisions are important shapers of their
thinking and strategies.

Other regional differences do not appear to be as significant in shaping
foundation work, although for many foundations, particularly in British
Columbia and the Prairies where there are large Indigenous communities,
both urban and non-urban, the presence and relationships of Indigenous
communities, and the importance of the work of reconciliation and decol-
onization has become much more central since 2015. The final report of
the Truth and Reconciliation Commission (TRC) and the philanthropic
community's *Declaration of Action* made in June 2015 to the TRC has
galvanized more philanthropic activity, as I describe in Chapter 9. While
there is still far to go, over the last few years there has been a heightened
awareness and interest in focusing more on reconciliation work with
Indigenous partners in a way that was unheard of before 2010.

In the chapters that follow, I have chosen to describe the work of the
individual foundations around seven themes or areas of focus: building
fields, strengthening community, shifting power, advancing public policy,
confronting climate change, partnering for impact, and building new
relationships with Indigenous peoples. In each case, I use the individual
stories both to illustrate the value that is contributed by these foundations,
and to reflect on the ways in which they have grappled with the pressures,
both internal and external, to be accountable, responsive, and flexible in
their strategies and behaviours. They are far from the only foundations
in Canada that are strategic and proactive in their work. There are many
more that could be mentioned. It is important to underline that the
foundations I chose for this book are a small segment of a much larger
field. Frankly, I would characterize them as outliers, not representatives.
Just as a handful of American foundations are better known than all
the rest, so these foundations in Canada, through their own efforts or the
voices of their partners, have become better known than the great majority
of their peers. Yet even though they are not typical, they are important as
examples of the variety and scope of philanthropic activity.

They share a progressive view of social change. Some, like the
McConnell Foundation, are nationally known because they have been
explicitly engaged in systemic change for decades. Others are better known
for the work in their chosen fields. In all cases they have been active for a
long enough period that the evolution of their strategies can be described.

And a key word applicable to their strategic evolution is "adaptability." Foundations are working in unstable times. The 2020–22 pandemic was a confirmation of the truth of this, as few other global events since the last world war have been. Climate change, or what is increasingly viewed as the climate emergency, is leading to even more disruption in our foreseeable future. In these times, adaptability is crucial. An effective strategy in philanthropy can't be too rigid or too specific. Indeed, as Dame Julia Unwin, a long-time British observer of philanthropic strategy, has said, "Strategy is a map not a set of instructions."[20] It can provide direction but not detail. Effective foundations check their compasses regularly. They adapt their work according to what is shifting around them and according to their own understanding of the outcomes. They cannot depend on fixed paths or certainties. "Every foundation should regularly ask itself these three questions," says Allan Northcott, president of the Max Bell Foundation of Calgary. "What are we trying to accomplish? Why are we trying to accomplish it? Why are we doing it that way?"[21]

Summarizing his views on strategy and the effectiveness of philanthropy, Phil Buchanan notes that "there are no magic apps, secret formulas, quick fixes, or one-size-fits-all frameworks."[22] But he also concludes, optimistically, that "effective giving can produce extraordinary results." I agree. In the following chapters I illustrate the work of Canadian foundations producing great value in the form of innovation, new thinking, and long-term investment in the development of solutions for our society and for our common future.

Building Fields

*The Counselling Foundation of Canada,
the Lawson Foundation, the Inspirit
Foundation, the McConnell Foundation*

Your task is not to foresee the future, but to enable it.

Antoine de Saint-Exupéry

Whom do I want to be when I grow up? How am I going to take my first steps into the world of work? How do I know what I am good at? These are questions that most young people face as they move from childhood into adulthood and from education into employment. In the 1950s in Canada, there weren't too many places where young people could go to find answers, especially if they didn't have families or older adults who could guide them. One of the places they could go was the local Y. The first YMCA in Canada was established in Montreal in 1851. By the 1950s, many Ys across Canada offered career and employment services as part of their mission to support the development of young people in mind, body, and spirit. Frank Lawson, a successful Toronto stockbroker, volunteered as a board member with the Toronto Y. In this role he got to know Dr Gerald Cosgrave, the director of the Toronto Y's counselling service, and a leading thinker in his day about career development. From this relationship was born a family's philanthropic commitment to build the field of career counselling in Canada, one that has had enormous impact on the career success of young people for over sixty years.

Frank Lawson's interest in career counselling came out of his own experience of being mentored as a young man, and his involvement as a mentor and volunteer with the Y. In the late 1950s, his vision, amplified by his contacts with Cosgrave, became larger. In 1950 he created a private foundation that he named not after himself, nor after his family, but after his passion: The Counselling Foundation of Canada. Influenced by Cosgrave, Lawson decided to put some of his ideas into action in the early

1960s by funding a pilot career counselling centre at Glendon College in northern Toronto. The importance of building this university-based centre was the opportunity to get recognition for career counselling as a professional field, and as a discipline in the field of applied psychology. According to his grandson Bruce Lawson, current president of The Counselling Foundation, Frank Lawson's vision was that career centres would be understood as an important part of a university campus because of their role in helping students fulfill their potential and apply their skills and talents to highest and best purposes. Ultimately, a great public good would be served. Employees would be happier, productivity would increase, and the economy would benefit. For Frank Lawson, career counselling had an important psychological dimension, not just a technical one. The goal of counselling young people at an early stage was to help strengthen their internal ability to understand what they were good at, and what they needed to do well, as well as to overcome negativity from others. He placed his bet on universities to invest in counselling platforms to deliver this help and to do it sustainably. In effect, he was willing to apply all his philanthropic resources to building a whole new field.

Is there a special role for foundations in field-building? How do you define field-building anyway? One way to describe it is bringing together various unconnected players to create more organized activity around an issue or set of issues. The work of field-building can cover any domain. Some examples of social change-oriented fields that have been built with philanthropic support include public health, justice reform, social finance, social entrepreneurship, climate adaptation and, yes, career development. Many large American foundations, such as Rockefeller, Gates, Skoll, and Ford, are field-builders. Judith Rodin, a former president of the Rockefeller Foundation, suggests that "a strength of philanthropy is our ability and legacy of creating, building, and defining entire fields."[1] Rodin goes on to say that not all fields are built deliberately. "Often philanthropy's greatest talent is in spotting a compelling idea, even if we don't fully understand it at the time, and giving it a chance to blossom."[2] Many, if not most foundations become field-builders because they want to try to make a difference in resolving complex social problems. The Bridgespan Group, a US philanthropic consulting firm, has studied philanthropic action to build fields and it describes this work as "meaningful, intentional coordination across a field's actors ... to elevate and sustain its collective practice."[3] The Bridgespan researchers who have examined philanthropic field-building identify five characteristics that serve as a solid foundation for a field: knowledge base, actors, field-level agenda, infrastructure, and resources.[4] To have impact at the population-level scale, Bridgespan suggests funders need to invest in all of these characteristics. They can invest in a field either through strengthening individual organizations or supporting collaboration among organizations and networks, or both.

Bridgespan makes a useful distinction between two categories of fields: those focused on a specific problem (e.g., achieving universal access to high-quality pre-kindergarten), and those focused on broad issue areas (e.g., early childhood).[5] Although it distinguishes these types, it also suggests that the work of field-building requires advancing both. For example, without raising broad support for investment in early childhood, it is more difficult to succeed in creating universal access to pre-kindergarten. This has been the experience of Canadian foundations interested in early childhood, such as the Margaret and Wallace McCain Family Foundation, or the Lawson Foundation, or the Atkinson Foundation, and the Lucie et André Chagnon Foundation, which have worked together to build the case for investing in early childhood while pressing for more specific changes in the supports available to very young children and their families. These foundations saw the value of collaboration years ago. Given the complexity and time necessary to build a field, most foundations doing this work find they need collaborators sooner or later.

Clearly, field-building takes time, sustained focus and commitment, and willingness to collaborate. Most foundations don't launch themselves knowingly into the demanding work of field-building. Yet, as Rodin pointed out, funders can pursue a compelling idea which only over time evolves into a body of work that builds a field. In this chapter I describe the evolution into field-builders of three private and one public foundation, each one of which has had an impact on the fields they have chosen. Over many decades, The Counselling Foundation of Canada has single-handedly professionalized the field of career counselling. The Lawson Foundation is a field-builder in two areas, early childhood development and diabetes prevention and treatment, linked by an overarching focus on the well-being of children and youth. The McConnell Foundation has been a field-builder since the 1990s in community-based economic development, social finance, and social innovation. The Inspirit Foundation is the newest funder, and it is leading in the effort to build the field of narrative change as a channel to promote its ultimate vision of pluralism, "a Canada where we can have tough conversations, but still feel like we all belong." Inspirit does this through focus areas that can change over time; in 2022 the focus is on combatting Islamophobia and fostering reconciliation with Indigenous Peoples. These funders have all taken risks to try different approaches and are sharing their learnings as they go.

The Counselling Foundation of Canada

Frank Lawson died in 1984, leaving a significant legacy to endow his foundation for the future. By the time of his death, the initial pilot career centre, which had moved to the main campus of York University, had been copied at other universities and community colleges with support from the foundation. Frank's son Donald and daughter Jean, as well as Donald's wife, Lorraine, joined the foundation board and began to formalize the newly endowed foundation with more defined goals and grantmaking policies. They were mentored by a career counselling professional, Elizabeth McTavish, who had directed the career centre at York and who became the foundation's first executive director. The next generation of the Lawson family remained committed to Frank Lawson's vision and built on it by expanding beyond career counselling at the post-secondary level to funding activities that supported the potential of youth outside of the university context.

Over the next two decades, the foundation began in small steps to build the field of counselling and of youth employment more broadly. It began to connect field actors through networks. For example, it invested in building a network for youth employment counselling centres across Ontario, which had previously worked independently and without a way to standardize and share practices. The foundation's investment created the Ontario Association of Youth Employment Centres (now known as First Work), an association that provides a platform for the centres to communicate and share with each other, while also engaging youth voices and advocating for more effective youth employment policies. Another investment by the foundation created an ongoing opportunity for career development professionals across the country to meet in an annual open conference. This investment in knowledge-building led to an important decision by The Counselling Foundation to create what was, in effect, an operating arm of the foundation, a charitable entity called CERIC (formerly known as the Canadian Education and Research Institute for Counselling). CERIC, which was created in 2001 and officially launched in 2004, evolved organically from a digital resource hub to a creator of career counselling-related research and content, a producer of publications and journals, the principal organizer of the annual professional development conference for career counsellors, and provider of support for graduate students whose academic focus is on career counselling.

The Counselling Foundation's ongoing funding for CERIC amounts to over $1 million per year. CERIC is now a national leader in career development. The relationship between the foundation and CERIC makes it a central focus of the foundation's work. Through CERIC, the foundation, which has a relatively small endowment and only three full-time staff, nevertheless has been able to extend its reach across Canada and to make a crucial difference to the field of career development and youth employment, and, consequently, to the lives of thousands of students. But this has not been the only contribution of The Counselling Foundation to field-building. According to Bruce Lawson, field-building has been a thread in the work of the foundation for over forty years. The family retains a majority presence on the board of the foundation with a family member as chair or vice-chair, and Bruce Lawson himself as the first family member to work on staff as president. The foundation has also consistently lent its support to field-building for the Canadian charitable sector, funding the operations of intermediary organizations such as Imagine Canada, PFC, and the Circle on Philanthropy and Aboriginal Peoples in Canada (the Circle).

Even more importantly, the foundation, under Bruce's leadership, took an original step in 2015 to create a physical meeting space for intermediaries. In partnership with two other private foundations (Lawson and Laidlaw), The Counselling Foundation created Foundation House, a unique collaborative working space in Toronto that houses not only the three foundations but also sector umbrella organizations such as Environment Funders Canada and the Ontario Nonprofit Network, as well as meeting and working spaces for PFC, Community Foundations of Canada, and the Circle. Foundation House has been enormously productive in building networks for the philanthropic sector in Canada. "The Foundation House experience has been seminal in fostering relationships and building connections," says Lawson.[6] From the beginning, the three foundations developed collaborative programming and curated regular exchanges among the leaders and staff of the organizations at Foundation House. This has contributed to daily collegiality and creative exchange. It also laid the groundwork for the three private foundations to support new collaborative funding initiatives, such as the Indigenous Peoples Resilience Fund, discussed in Chapter 9.

The foundation recommitted itself to the work of building the field for career development in its 2020 strategic plan. After many decades of investment, it fully recognizes that the field is multi-dimensional and that various sub-fields cross-cut and overlap each other. As Bridgespan points out in its report on field-building, if these sub-fields are not unified by a philanthropic focus on the larger field, they end up competing for scarce resources. The Counselling Foundation identifies the larger field of career development as its primary focus, with commitments in four sub-fields that together contribute to advancing the broad field. The four areas in which the foundation works now are: youth leadership and youth empowerment, workforce development, employability skills and competency awareness, and Indigenous youth career transitions.[7] In restating its commitment to this field, the foundation has also articulated its philosophy as a field-building funder, one that could serve as a statement for other foundation peers in this work: "Continued success in this work requires deep commitment to partnerships, collaborations and the engagement of those representing the communities [the Foundation] seeks to serve ... the Foundation works with organizations and their leaders who have the vision and drive to make change happen not just today but for the years even generations ahead. This means accepting that even the best-sounding ideas come with risks, and success – however it is measured – is not guaranteed and may not be well-defined. The Foundation can and will make these decisions, learn from them and work with others to share this knowledge."[8]

The Lawson Foundation

One of Bruce Lawson's neighbours and foundation colleagues at Foundation House is Marcel Lauzière, president of the Lawson Foundation. There is no relation between the Lawson family of The Counselling Foundation and the Lawsons of the Lawson Foundation. Unlike Bruce, Marcel is not a member of the family. But Marcel and Bruce have many other things in common. Marcel, like Bruce, leads a multi-generational foundation with many family members still very engaged through the board of directors. Both foundations were started in the late 1950s by successful businessmen who used the foundation as a personal philanthropic vehicle. Their children and spouses took over the governance of their fathers' foundations and it is now the third, fourth, and fifth generations of the families who are directors of what have become institutional philanthropic vehicles. Both foundations share an interest in youth development, although the

Lawson Foundation positions itself as an investor in early childhood and in healthy development of children and youth, while The Counselling Foundation is engaged in supporting older youth and young adults. Both foundations invest in strengthening the charitable sector and are collaborative creators (along with the Laidlaw Foundation) of Foundation House. And both foundations have acted as field-builders, even though they may not have been so firmly set in this role when they began their work sixty or more years ago.

The Lawson Foundation was created in 1956 by the Honourable Ray Lawson, a distinguished business leader in London and Toronto, Ontario. Through to the 1990s, the foundation was led by Ray (who died in 1980) and his children Tom and Ruth, who supported many local organizations, particularly in London where they lived. The third generation of the family in the 1990s began to play a role on the board and in shaping the strategy of the foundation, which focused on two principal areas, early child development and diabetes treatment, both of which emerged out of the personal interests and experiences of the third generation. The foundation took on a professional executive director in the 1990s and formalized its practices as a grantmaker, becoming one of the few Canadian foundations to become active in the US-based National Center for Family Philanthropy at a time before the creation of Canadian philanthropic networks. As the years passed and more of the fourth generation arrived on the board, the foundation became sharper in its focus while retaining its priority activity in early childhood and diabetes. But it was not yet seeing itself as a field-builder, although it collaborated with other funders in advocating for public policy changes in the field of early childhood education, and funded research in both fields that contributed to an important shared knowledge base.

The major shift into a field-building role began in 2014 when the Lawson Foundation hired Marcel Lauzière as president. Lauzière had deep experience in leading the charitable sector, as former president of Imagine Canada. He worked with the foundation's board, which comprised both fourth-generation family members and independent directors by this stage, to articulate a new strategic direction that would strengthen its focus on children and youth and take Lawson to the next level. The foundation was still deeply committed to early childhood development and diabetes prevention. But for the first time it connected its work to the broader field of the healthy development of children and youth. It identified three interrelated sub-fields in which it would work: early child development, healthy active children and youth, and youth and the environment. It decided to fold its diabetes prevention and treatment work into its focus on healthy living behaviours, which are often learned in childhood. This thinking was consistent with the understanding that successful field-building requires work on both problem-based fields, such as diabetes prevention, and broader issue fields, such as healthy child development.

As the foundation began to implement its new strategic direction, it launched a multi-year Outdoor Play Strategy and a Child and Youth Diabetes Strategy. It also adopted an approach that fits into the frame of field-building. Lawson had funded the knowledge base in its areas of interest well before 2015 through its commitments to academic and practical research. After 2015, Lawson pursued its strategies with the addition of funding for the "actors" in its chosen fields to learn from each other. It brought together cohorts of organizations working in the areas of outdoor play and child and youth diabetes, and youth involved in action on the environment to participate together in the exchange of lessons and practices. According to Lauzière, "the organizations [we fund under our strategies] have to agree to be part of a cohort … to mentor and learn from each other." The foundation brings the cohorts together at least once or twice a year. From this, says Lauzière, "we have a lot of learning. Our first cohort in outdoor play [for example] taught us that the expectations of the foundation were not clear enough at the beginning … and they have learned that their cohorts can provide truly helpful advice especially in the last year or two of a strategy."[9] The organizations in the cohort also help each other to build a field-level agenda, which Bridgespan defines as an overarching strategy of approaches that field actors pursue to address barriers and develop adaptive solutions.[10]

The foundation has learned through its cohort work to listen more carefully to the views and perspectives of field actors. Lauzière and his staff of six feel themselves to be accountable to their grantees for clear and timely communication and for flexibility in responding to the issues of each organization. Lauzière comments that it is important for the foundation to "commit to opening doors and making connections to help grantees do their work." This approach has served the Lawson Foundation well in its response to the 2020–22 pandemic, and to a shift to more trust-based and adaptive philanthropy. It is also an illustration of how the foundation thinks broadly about building a field through all the resources that it brings, including not only convening and public policy advocacy, but also the deployment of its assets through impact investing. In 2020, as part of its commitment to a process of reconciliation with Indigenous Peoples, the foundation tightened its diabetes focus further to address the Type 2 diabetes epidemic in Indigenous northern and remote communities with a ten-year strategy. To tackle this difficult challenge, and to act on its commitment to community-led action, the foundation added to its funding and convening tools with an innovative investing approach. In 2019, it co-funded with the federal government an Indigenous-led Solutions Lab process to identify community-driven diabetes prevention and management interventions. This is leading to the development of a community-driven outcomes contract to finance diabetes reduction initiatives identified by the lab and initiated by an Indigenous-led investment fund, Raven Indigenous Capital Partners.

The Lawson Foundation has also committed itself to helping to build field infrastructure. In each of the fields where it works, it has created or supported network organizations bringing together many of its grantees. Diabetes Canada, Outdoor Play Canada, the Canadian Child Care Federation are all examples of these types of networks. In addition, and very much like its partner The Counselling Foundation, Lawson sustains the major philanthropic field networks in Canada, including Imagine Canada, PFC, Environment Funders Canada, and regional networks such as the Ontario Nonprofit Network and Pillar Nonprofit Network (in London). With Counselling and Laidlaw, it contributed funds to the Indigenous Peoples Resilience Fund in 2020 as well as to the new Foundation for Black Communities. This kind of funding, while unusual for private foundations, is aligned with Lauzière's own experience and beliefs. As a former leader of Imagine Canada, he is aware of the importance of the field infrastructure that underpins the non-profit sector's professional development, public policy, and advocacy work.

Finally, as a field-builder, the Lawson Foundation has acted on a commitment to bring resources to the mobilization of knowledge. Since 2015 it has invested in developmental evaluations of its major strategies which it has made available to its peers and the wider field. It shares full information on its grants, including not only the recipients but also the purposes of each grant. And it has been a field-builder for other families in philanthropy. The Lawson Foundation is now working with the fifth generation of what has become a large extended family. While family foundations rarely offer public details about their practices for integrating new generations of the family into the work of philanthropy, the Lawson Foundation has willingly done so, openly sharing its structured approach to introducing younger members to grantmaking and to the goals and strategies of a family foundation. As a field-builder, Lawson has unquestionably extended the impact of its work while remaining very much in the spirit of the philanthropic interest of the early generations.

The Inspirit Foundation

My next example of philanthropic field-building moves away from the world of family-governed foundations. The Inspirit Foundation is a public foundation based in Toronto. It emerged as a charitable entity between 2010 and 2012 out of a Canadian television network, Vision TV, which was dedicated to multi-faith programming. The sale of Vision TV provided assets that created a foundation initially known as S-Vox and then, from 2012 on, as Inspirit. The foundation's mission at the beginning was to promote the inclusion of all in a pluralist, multicultural Canada, based on the legacy of Vision TV, which made space for Canadians from all faith groups to tell their stories. Inspirit's mission now explicitly spells out how its promotion of inclusion and pluralism will take place "through media and arts, support for young content creators, and impact investing – specifically addressing discrimination based on ethnicity, race or religion."

Sadia Zaman, the chief executive officer of Inspirit, came to the foundation in 2018, leaving a career built around television and media. A trained journalist, she had worked for Vision TV as a director of in-house production before moving on to run a national non-profit for women in film and television and then taking on a senior role at the Canadian Broadcasting Corporation. Under her leadership, Inspirit has returned to its origin story in Vision TV, more specifically to narrative change, a fledgling field in Canada. She explains that "at the heart of what we were doing [at Vision TV] was challenging how we were and are portrayed and how that affects policy, how people see us, how we see ourselves as members of a pluralistic society."[11] Her commitment to Vision's mission was a commitment, in her words, to the "important but challenging idea of how a multicultural country learns to live in a way that ensures we all belong." The foundation supports young content creators who want to tell their own stories and those of their communities, specifically communities enduring discrimination on racial, ethnic, or religious grounds. Its funding increases the production and amplification of diverse narratives. Narratives are important as collections of stories that shape people's behaviours and opinions, as well as the policies that affect their lives. As Zaman puts it, "narratives have the ability to foster understanding, elicit empathy and catalyze change." The foundation has focused on narratives led by Indigenous Peoples to foster narrative sovereignty and is building infrastructure to support stories told by Canadian Muslims. Speaking of their work with Indigenous communities, Zaman says, "We hope to increase the production, exposure, and amplification of Indigenous narratives, as well as to develop skills and resources within Indigenous communities to tell their own stories."

Inspirit is taking the lead in Canada in building a field around narrative change. Their initiative is unique but inspired by American foundations using narrative change to challenge racial injustice in the United States, such as the Pillars Fund, a Muslim philanthropic foundation that focuses on narratives by American Muslims. Inspirit is using philanthropic resources to support field actors and create infrastructure for narrative. In the fall of 2020, the foundation launched its Narrative Change Lab as an experiment to support practitioners and content creators from underrepresented communities who want to advance the narratives of Black and Indigenous Peoples as well as people of colour. Realizing that it needed to take the time to do some deep thinking about how narratives develop, and the role of a funder in this work, Inspirit hired a full-time program manager working in collaboration with a foundation fellow, a knowledgeable Muslim journalist, to research and develop the inaugural Narrative Change Lab. In 2021 it focused the work of the Change Lab on narratives by Muslims in Canada, with the goal of supporting narratives that move beyond trauma to the many stories Muslim content creators want to tell through film, documentary, comedy, and journalism. The foundation believes the presence and amplification of these diverse narratives in the pop culture landscape is what will challenge the media stereotypes that have had very real consequences for Muslims. In 2022, the Change Lab is convening a cohort of Muslim leaders in arts and media to explore the various issues affecting Muslims in Canada, focusing especially on the intersections of narratives and pop culture. The work is evolving as the conversations continue. Says Zaman, "We are thinking through what could be most helpful. A theme that keeps coming up is that of power ... those who control the purse strings control the narrative."

The Change Lab is posing a challenging question: "How can a narrative change model factor in power in a way that results in narrative building power for people?" Zaman says, "We want to bring together folks to think about that and other questions emerging from our research." She and her colleagues are not prescribing the timetable. They are taking the time to let the process evolve and to generate initiatives that Inspirit could fund. As the Lawson and Counselling foundations have learned in their own work, a commitment to field-building takes a willingness to listen to the actors and patience to allow the most effective ideas and initiatives to emerge through knowledge-building, connections, and time. Time is as valuable an asset as money in the work of field-building, and it is an asset uniquely available to foundations, whether private or public.

The McConnell Foundation

The McConnell Foundation is my fourth example of philanthropic field-building. This is one of the better-known private foundations in Canada. Like the first two foundations in this chapter, it is a family foundation and it is governed by fourth and fifth generations of the McConnell family. First established as a personal philanthropic vehicle by business leader J.W. McConnell in Montreal in the late 1930s, it operated for its first fifty years as a traditional funder of charitable institutions, mostly, but not exclusively, in Montreal. Jack McConnell, as he was known to his family and friends, played a central role in the development of many of Montreal's English institutions, including the major anglophone hospitals, McGill University, the Montreal YMCA, and other community social service clubs and organizations. After the death of J.W. McConnell, in 1964, the foundation, formally renamed the J.W. McConnell Family Foundation, continued to be governed by family members and managed by the family office. Its philanthropy also continued in the pattern set by Jack McConnell, who had been the principal philanthropic decision-maker during his lifetime.

The McConnell endowment grew significantly after Jack McConnell's death. By the time the third generation of the family on the board chose Tim Brodhead in 1993 as the first arms-length non-family staff leader of the foundation, its endowment was the largest of a private family foundation in Canada. And it was ready to think very differently about its role. Brodhead himself did not come out of philanthropy, although his roots were in Montreal. His experience had been on the grant-seeking side. Before joining McConnell as president, he had spent his career in international development, and he came to the foundation from the leadership of an umbrella network for Canadian international non-governmental organizations, the Canadian Council for International Cooperation (now known as Cooperation Canada). He had a broader vision of the national possibilities for a large grantmaking foundation. And the third-generation McConnell board members were receptive. Together they decided on a strategy that was a significant change from the institution-building, grantee-by-grantee approach that McConnell was known for previously.

The foundation decided it wanted to fund issues, ones that were material and nationally significant. The issue it chose first was an ambitious one: how to foster more dynamic regional economies across the country. Stronger regional- or community-level capacity was needed, according to regional development experts. But there was no obvious national backbone for strengthening community development at a local level. To begin designing a program, the foundation convened two dozen or so people involved in local community development. It asked them a provocative question: Rather than *each* of you receiving an individual grant, what would *all* of you benefit from to do your work? People agreed they all wanted technical expertise that they could hire for their local needs. If their communities had more of this expertise, they would have the power in their hands to understand and develop their own opportunities. This answer led the foundation to a new solution: to fund a program called the Community Economic Development Technical Assistance Program (CEDTAP), under the guidance of Ted Jackson at Carleton University.

McConnell learned a valuable lesson from CEDTAP about how to work with an intermediary or backbone organization. The foundation structured its funding so it went to the backbone (CEDTAP); the users of CEDTAP services did not have to worry about the value of what they were contracting for since CEDTAP itself could test the expertise. One of the reasons why CEDTAP as an intermediary was so important in the mid-1990s was that governments were withdrawing from the community development field because of austerity measures and spending cuts. Gaps in policy development and pilot testing were not being readily filled by other sources. Private foundations like McConnell could and did step in. By partnering with an academic institution (Carleton) to deliver an initiative for a community to strengthen its capacities, the foundation gained more than the sum of its parts.

The framing of this initiative gave McConnell a starting point for much of its field-building work going forward. It was able to move funds to hundreds more beneficiaries through the intermediary than it could on its own. And communities were helped to determine their priorities through a semi-facilitated process that McConnell could not have delivered itself. The work on CEDTAP led to an important investment by McConnell in a program called Vibrant Communities, a collective-impact approach introduced to over a hundred communities across Canada working on poverty reduction and anti-poverty strategies. The backbone intermediary in this case was the Tamarack Institute. Tamarack was created in 2001 out of conversations between Alan Broadbent, chair of the Maytree Foundation of Toronto, and Paul Born, an anti-poverty activist. Broadbent and Born drew in Tim Brodhead and the McConnell Foundation as allies in the effort to create a collaborative, cross-sectoral approach to local poverty reduction in cities. Tamarack's experience shows the evolution of the model from an intermediary working one-on-one in communities to an intermediary supporting a learning community backed by evaluators and researchers (particularly at the Caledon Institute, also funded by Maytree) who distill and share lessons and resources and contribute to conversations with public policy makers. Maytree and McConnell made a sustained multi-year funding commitment to Tamarack and Vibrant Communities. This has resulted in a remarkable field-building contribution to reducing poverty and deepening communities across Canada.[12]

Through the 2000s, McConnell followed this approach to field-building in multiple issue areas. In the area of immigrant employment, it partnered with Maytree again to create a national intermediary program called ALLIES (Assisting Local Leaders with Immigrant Employment Strategies) with the goal of creating a multi-sectoral network for spreading best practices in immigrant employment from one city to another across Canada. In the area of disability rights, McConnell supported the Planned Lifetime Advocacy Network (PLAN), an organization that serves people with disabilities and their families. McConnell's funding enabled PLAN to create a national network to serve, advocate for, and connect people with disabilities. In the area of caregiving, McConnell supported the Canadian Caregiver Coalition, which was inspired by PLAN's work to create new systemic supports for caregivers, such as allowances and tax credits.

McConnell also paid attention to infrastructure as part of its field-building work. This attention came naturally to Brodhead, who had led a national network, and who participated actively in other national sector networks such as the Voluntary Sector Roundtable in the mid-1990s. Like the Counselling and Lawson foundations, McConnell has funded the national philanthropy umbrellas such as Imagine Canada and PFC. It also funded infrastructure development at sub-sectoral levels, such as the Strathmere Group, which helped national environmental organizations collaborate on policy and strategy around climate change and the impact of the development of the oil sands. Knowing that change takes time, the foundation, in most cases, made multi-year funding commitments to infrastructure, and to the organizations and networks it supported in the multiple fields it chose to work in.

Even in the early days of field-building, the foundation had asked itself how it could spark and systematize ideas and learnings. It took on an active role as convener of various actors in the fields it entered. Like the Lawson Foundation, it brought cohorts of grantees together to talk about their work and share practices. It invested in developmental evaluations. And it commissioned and published narrative stories about the fields in which it chose to intervene. Many of the foundation's investments were shaped by its interest in social entrepreneurs and social innovation. The foundation created an Applied Dissemination initiative, which brought together a group of diverse grantees working on bringing their innovations to scale. In 2006, Brodhead articulated McConnell's thinking in a speech to the foundation's partners: "It is up to funders, and especially private foundations with their greater flexibility and tolerance for risk, to actively help our social entrepreneurs by welcoming promising new ideas, giving them the time and resources to test their efficacy, and helping to link them to funders, investors, policy-makers and partners so that innovation powers social progress no less than economic prosperity."[13]

To "create an *ecology*," in its words, for this type of innovation, the foundation, in 2007, partnered with the MaRS Discovery District in Toronto, the University of Waterloo, and the PLAN Institute in Vancouver to establish Social Innovation Generation (SiG). The goals of SiG were to build capacity, mobilize capital, and create a culture in support of continuous social innovation. In 2011, the foundation helped the University of Waterloo launch a graduate diploma program in social innovation. Recognizing that the field of social finance and impact investing was still very undeveloped, in 2010 McConnell, through SiG, launched the Task Force on Social Finance made up of Canadian business and community leaders (including Brodhead) to make recommendations to promote impact investing so as to (in the words of the task force report) "mobilize private capital for the public good." The report of this task force had a significant impact on the investment strategies of private foundations in Canada, who, for the first time, were challenged to meet a target of up to 10 per cent of their portfolios in impact investments by 2020.[14]

McConnell's comprehensive approach to accelerating social change was distilled in 2008 in a prescient document *Accelerating our Impact: Philanthropy, Innovation and Social Change* written by Katharine Pearson, the social innovation director at the foundation. In this paper, she described the broad-scale social change activities of the foundation in terms that evoke Bridgehead's definition of field-building:

- mobilizing and brokering relevant knowledge among researchers and practitioners
- convening individuals and groups with a common purpose across sectors to generate learning and collaboration
- developing leadership capacity for social change
- offering systems transformation (such as skills development, coaching, and fund diversification strategies)[15]

She concluded, in a summary that captures the essence of field-building work by foundations and by other collaborators and partners and echoes the words of The Counselling Foundation of Canada: "Through taking risks, harnessing resources, sticking with change processes over time, investing in leadership, collaborating, tracking, adjusting, and communicating, we have seen brilliant, but isolated experiments become widely accepted and practiced. ... Innovative leaders also need relevant and timely research, customized training, and the opportunity to forge alliances with influential individuals, institutions, and organizations. Most of all, they need unflinching support to enable them to explore and make mistakes. These processes are essential to learning, to the discovery of new and lasting solutions to chronic problems, and to the pursuit of the sustainable world to which we are all committed."[16] In the next chapter, I continue the story of the McConnell Foundation as I look more closely at the approach to building community assets at the local level.

Strengthening Community

The Metcalf Foundation, the McConnell Foundation, the Atkinson Foundation

The impact of our grant-making is strengthened when grounded in community and collaboration, complemented through our leadership in capacity-building, reinforced with policy analysis and augmented through partnerships that focus on systems change.

Metcalf Foundation Biennial Report 2016–17

How does a private foundation go about tackling a deep-rooted problem like neighbourhood poverty? In 1998, this difficult question confronted the board of the Metcalf Foundation of Toronto. The Metcalf Foundation is named after its founder, George Cedric Metcalf, a highly successful business leader in the 1950s and 1960s with a career in the food business, running George Weston Ltd and Loblaw. In 1960, like many of his peers, he created a foundation as a vehicle for his personal philanthropy and community engagement. But he was too busy to run it. Johanna and George Metcalf, daughter-in-law and son of George Cedric, took on that responsibility as a couple and as board members of the foundation in the early 1980s. The family members followed their philanthropic interests. George the son and Johanna were interested in the arts and supported a range of social service, health, and education programs. George Metcalf the son died before his father, in 1990. Eight years later, George Cedric Metcalf died, leaving a very large legacy to the foundation that bore his name.

The board of the Metcalf Foundation in the 1990s was steered by Johanna Metcalf and her three children, the grandchildren of George Cedric. Johanna had a strong commitment to social justice as well as an ongoing passion for the arts. The family directed donations toward organizations working in the areas of food security, child poverty, and literacy, as well as the performing arts. The financial legacy of George

Cedric Metcalf, which came into the foundation endowment in 1998, was a tipping point; the $110 million it represented turned Metcalf overnight into one of the largest foundations in Canada in the early 2000s. Alexander (Sandy) Houston, a lawyer who was newly appointed as president of the foundation, worked with the Metcalf board on developing a strategic approach to the challenge of deploying their new endowment. They began a five-year long reflection on their goals and strategies, asking themselves some searching questions: What should we do and why? How should we do it? Where can we be most helpful? How will we know? How can we best contribute to helping people and organizations to build a "just, healthy and creative society"[1] in Canada? By 2004–05 they had developed programs for their three broad funding areas: the performing arts, the environment, and poverty reduction, focusing largely on southern Ontario and the city of Toronto.

The challenge they were setting for themselves on poverty reduction was enormous. Persistent poverty in neighbourhoods is a complex social and economic problem that is very hard to solve. Lengthy books have been written on this topic. For foundations, there is appeal in trying to tackle poverty in their own geographic communities, where the problems and solutions are closer to hand. Place-based philanthropy or community development philanthropy are descriptions used for these local poverty reduction strategies. Some strategies redefine the problem not as a deficit of assets in communities but as an issue of mobilization of existing assets. A low-income neighbourhood may not possess financial assets but it often has other assets such as people with skills, organizations with a base in the community, physical assets such as land, and human capital such as labour. What the community needs to develop these assets is support for skills and leadership development, forging partnerships and connections, and help with removal of policy or legal barriers. This thinking suggests that philanthropy's best strategy is to "recognize the strengths, gifts, talents and resources of individuals and communities, and to help communities to mobilize and build on these for sustainable development. … At the core [of this strategy] are the various assets (human, social, financial, natural, and physical) that already exist in the community, especially the formal and informal associations that mobilize assets and strengthen the social relationships that are important for bridging local initiatives to external opportunities."[2] Dr Phillips, in a 2018 study[3] of place-based philanthropy, has provided a typology of philanthropic approaches to community building that includes five models that capture aspects of asset-based community development: collective impact, community wealth building, capacity building, impact investing, and horizontal community philanthropy, or grassroots empowerment. In each of these models she suggests that community or private foundations can add value to a local community in various ways that build out from grantmaking to advancing social innovation, building constituencies and capacities, shaping ideas and agenda setting, and advocating for policy and social change.

In this chapter, I trace the evolving strategies of two private foundations, Metcalf in Toronto, and McConnell in Montreal, that have been involved in community development work in their respective communities for decades. Many private foundations in Canada invest in their community to pursue strategies for poverty reduction. In this work, Metcalf and McConnell are far from alone. But over time, the strategies of these foundations have shifted considerably. Metcalf and McConnell began by funding community organizations directly but have broadened their approach to add many of the tools suggested by Phillips, while actively seeking or creating collaborations with other funders and neighbourhood leaders. I conclude the chapter with a description of the work of the Atkinson Foundation, a private foundation based in Toronto, that is focused on the intersection of racial and economic justice in Ontario and building opportunities for decent work in a fair economy.

The Metcalf Foundation and Toronto

Since 2004–05, the Metcalf Foundation has narrated its sixty-year story, shared its learnings, and documented its strategies in a remarkably detailed series of biennial reports representing a public narrative equalled by few other private foundations in Canada. Read together, these reports demonstrate the shift over two decades from a foundation supporting individuals and organizations in siloed projects to a foundation working in partnership and convening many different actors across fields to bring about sustainable and inclusive change for communities. These reports describe the evolution of the Metcalf Foundation's approach to building what it calls inclusive local economies.

The family brought its values and culture to the table in planning this work with its advisers and board members. According to Sandy Houston,

Metcalf's president, the family was humble in acknowledging what it could and couldn't do from the beginning. "They had no interest in telling other people what they should do," he says. "Their approach began with the precept 'first, do no harm.' They wanted to be enabling, supportive, intelligent but not directive."[4] They had an inquisitive approach, seeking expertise and advice from those with the answers. With help from their advisory committees, who were drawn from the communities they wished to serve, they chose grants where they felt the foundation could bolster or amplify the work being done by their grantees. They were prepared to use their funds creatively. They were willing to take risks and were comfortable being "early" on issues or approaches. For them, "learning by doing" was natural.

In its first biennial report, issued in 2005, the foundation set out a clear goal for its poverty work: "To enrich the development of strong community voices and comprehensive, collaborative long-term approaches to issues of poverty in Toronto." A continuing interest in supporting the voice and capacity of community leaders was the connecting thread weaving together its funding choices. It was prepared to do this in innovative ways. Metcalf's long-term poverty reduction efforts were delivered through what it called a Community Program with two streams: Communities in Action and Leadership in Action. Through this program, it supported people and organizations in low-income neighbourhoods. Focusing initially on income security policy reform as an answer to poverty, Metcalf built coalitions, funded policy research, and helped local organizations provide input to public policy development. It also provided support to ninety-eight emerging local leaders who were trained through a management and leadership program offered by York University.

In 2010, Metcalf made an important shift. It decided to focus on how to generate economic opportunities for low-income people. The foundation program that was eventually called Inclusive Local Economies was built on the initial work the foundation did on poverty reduction in the Greater Toronto Area. The change was to centre it on increasing access to labour markets and the creation of good jobs for low-income people, while retaining many of the elements of the previous place-based approach grounded in building the capacities of neighbourhood leaders and organizations. The foundation wanted to help communities explore economic tools for amplifying income as a way out of poverty. The question Metcalf was seeking to answer was: "What can be done at neighbourhood level to support access, entry and mobility in the labour market to make a living wage?" Learning as it went, and with much input from advisers and residents, in 2010 the foundation launched a pilot Resilient Neighbourhood Economies (RNE) project with two neighbourhoods in Toronto and three non-profit organizations working within those neighbourhoods: East Scarborough and Thorncliffe Park. The foundation saw itself as a partner with the non-profit organizations, not just a funder, and equally accountable for what worked and what didn't in the project. It "sharpened our understanding of our limitations and strengths ... and our sense of how best to contribute to the work" says Houston. Winding up the RNE project after three years, and building on its learnings, in 2012 Metcalf initiated the Inclusive Local Economies (ILE) program. The ILE program is based on three priorities: increasing access to quality jobs, protecting precarious workers, and strengthening local economies. The foundation continued to support local leaders and organizations working in East Scarborough, Thorncliffe Park, and Parkdale, because it had learned that it takes years for communities and effective strategies to coalesce, test approaches and adapt the lessons that emerge, and, ultimately, to develop a shared analysis focused on systemic rather than programmatic issues. Metcalf is deploying its assets in the neighbourhoods through both grants and impact investments. For example, its impact investments have helped the Parkdale Neighbourhood Land Trust to acquire and make available affordable housing units in the community.

According to Houston, one important role that Metcalf plays is as a convenor of learning spaces in the communities. Foundations, in his view, have a unique opportunity to augment impact through "connecting people and projects that have shared purposes but that aren't aware of each other or don't know each other." Doing the convening around themes is also enormously valuable. As Houston notes, "There isn't enough time or opportunity for people to participate in these valuable exchanges in their daily work." Metcalf funded and organized two gatherings of participants in the ILE program. From these gatherings and from its own evaluations, Metcalf learned how to better focus its efforts – and was able to build a shared analysis of issues and approaches with its partners.

In the next stage of its work, Metcalf continued to evolve. "The more involved we got in workforce development," says Houston, "the clearer it became that many low-income people are not well served by the current system. There are many barriers to workforce integration." Despite best intentions, the labour market was neither meeting employer needs nor providing the support and opportunities needed by jobseekers. Since a good job is the potent response to endemic poverty, Metcalf and its community partners asked some important questions: Why isn't the labour market working better? How should workers be prepared for successful entry? How do they enter? How can workforce development resources be used more effectively? Building on its earlier training work with hospitality sector workers in Toronto, and its experience in creating learning cohorts, Metcalf decided to experiment by partnering with the Aspen Institute. Aspen had developed and delivered a National Sector Skills Academy in the United States. This was a cohort-based fellowship program focused on improving the quantity, quality, and sustainability of systems-based workforce development efforts. Metcalf and Aspen adapted the model for a Canadian audience and for the local context. In 2016, Metcalf, with the support of The Counselling Foundation of Canada, delivered a Toronto Sector Skills Academy (TSSA). In the TSSA, Metcalf applied the learning it had accumulated from its work with the ILE program, focusing on convening a cohort of people, both community grassroots leaders and government policy partners, over ten months to build a shared vocabulary and tools around workforce development systems and opportunities to improve them. Two cohorts of participants benefited from the TSSA before the pandemic delayed further work.

Over the same period, the ILE program was bolstered by the involvement of two Metcalf Innovation fellows, Tom Zizys and Danielle Olsen, who produced research and wrote reports on crucial aspects of the workforce system in Ontario. Metcalf is also doing more collaborative work with other funders. In 2018, Metcalf and the JPMorgan Chase Foundation, which has a strong interest in workforce development, initiated the Toronto Workforce Funder Collaborative, a first in Canada. Seven funders (private, public, and corporate) are committed to learning and investing together in strategies to bring about more access to better jobs. The collaborative is supported by an executive director and has funded three community organizations in Toronto, testing and implementing partnerships to address root causes of local workforce challenges. It is working on a second round of funding to organizations working on employer engagement strategies.

All along, Metcalf has stayed true to the spirit and values of the Metcalf family, three of whom are still on the board. Their curiosity, combined with humility and patience, as well as their taste for learning, has permitted the foundation to develop its strategies organically. Over the years, the three areas of interest of the family, while still present in distinct programs, have also benefited from continuous learning and cross-pollination. Houston believes that the learning from the local economies work has percolated across the foundation's other areas of work in environment and the performing arts, just as the staff for each of these areas have learned from and work with each other. Metcalf has also come to understand the importance of a longer time horizon. "Too often we foundations are drawn to the next new thing or shift to a new approach too soon," concludes Houston. "Change is a slow and bumpy process and requires us to be patient, dogged and responsive. We should probably spend more of our time examining what we have done (good or bad) and make the needed adjustments." After twenty years, Metcalf would say it is still only at the beginning of investing in neighbourhood leaders, ideas, innovation, and networks in ways that will make a sustained difference to the lives and opportunities of low-income Torontonians.

The McConnell Foundation and Montreal

The McConnell Foundation is best known across Canada as a national funder. Yet the history of McConnell is closely bound up with the City of Montreal. The foundation has long supported key community institutions in education, health, and services to low-income, young, mentally ill, and/ or homeless citizens of Montreal. In the 1980s, the foundation shifted its attention to a national landscape, as described in the preceding chapter. Some of the local organizations it funded in Montreal inevitably became anxious about its commitment to its home community (although many of the family trustees continued to support Montreal institutions through their own directed grants). In the 1990s, McConnell decided to re-invest in Montreal institution building, this time to support infrastructure for community-wide institutional funders such as the United Way/Centraide of Greater Montreal (Centraide) and the Community Foundation of Greater Montreal. The Community Foundation was launched in 2000 with an endowment gift from McConnell and a good deal of brokering by Tim Brodhead, the leader of McConnell, behind the scenes. McConnell's funding of key infrastructure for Centraide, such as information tech-nology, staff training, and other capital investments, was critical to its strategic and philanthropic leap forward in the first decade of the 2000s. McConnell also made funding available to organizations facing a collective challenge, such as the independent libraries of Montreal, which were facing funding challenges and needed help in learning how to collaborate more and to explore alternative business models. At the same time, it reduced its grants to individual local organizations that had received McConnell support in the 1980s.

This strategy changed around 2015 when the City of Montreal was experiencing an economic and social low point with slow growth, allegations of municipal corruption, and crumbling infrastructure. Stephen Huddart, who had replaced Tim Brodhead as president in 2011, had been deeply involved in McConnell's effort through the 2000s to develop social innovation thinking and practices. Using this experience, he and the McConnell board decided to play a city-wide community rebuilding role focusing on innovation. The foundation convened voices from business, the arts, education, municipal governments, and others to participate in a continuing series of multi-sectoral civic conversations under the banner of Amplifier/Amplify Montreal. The conversations, and study tours to other cities such as New York, Chicago, London, and Bilbao to learn about their re-imagination of public civic spaces, gave Montreal's leaders renewed confidence and created new connections and networks among the innovators and builders of the city. McConnell's convening work led to its funding of a collaboration with an influential private sector leader in Montreal, Jacques Ménard of the Bank of Montreal, who had fostered a networking effort in 2013 called Je Vois (I See) Montreal. Je Vois Montreal boosted the work of a new interdisciplinary research centre at McGill University dedicated to the study of Montreal, which drew McConnell funding for its academic research. Je Vois Montreal led to the creation of Je Fais (I Build) MTL, a permanent forum in the City of Montreal, also funded in part by McConnell. The foundation invested with other partners including a B-Corporation[5] real estate developer and McGill University to pursue an idea, germinated by Je Fais MTL, to buy and repurpose a former Catholic church in south-west Montreal into Le Salon 1861, a new collaborative and meeting space for social innovators, entrepreneurs, artists, students, and community organizations.

McConnell's participation in these various city-building initiatives and conversations created a renewed presence for the foundation in its home city. It began to join in collaborative efforts with other major foundations in the city, including the Lucie et André Chagnon Foundation and the Mirella & Lino Saputo Foundation. McConnell had started a new national program in 2016, Cities for People, focused on developing an approach to helping cities to become more equitable, more inclusive, and more innovative. In Montreal, McConnell decided to channel its learnings from Cities for People into local initiatives. In late 2016, it collaborated with the Saputo Foundation and with three Montreal universities to launch the Maison de l'innovation sociale (the MIS) as a laboratory to research and facilitate the development of projects with a social impact, including urban innovation in Montreal. McConnell married its national and local roles in partnering with the MIS and others to found Future Cities Canada, a national collaborative platform to share ideas about building resilient, equitable, and sustainable urban infrastructure.

These initiatives for and with Montreal were very much driven by McConnell's particular interest in social innovation. In this sense, they were "grasstop" rather than "grassroots" projects. In 2015, McConnell took a step toward more locally driven work by joining a new collective impact funding project organized by the Chagnon Foundation and Centraide of Greater Montreal. This collaborative philanthropic model for community building, moving into its seventh year in 2022, involves nine foundations working together through Centraide to support and accelerate change at the local level with the goal of reducing poverty. The Collective Impact Project (CIP) is unusual in that it brings together a group of philanthropic partners, almost all of them private foundations, to pool funds and form a learning network facilitated by Centraide to understand more about what works and what doesn't in local efforts to strengthen low-income neighbourhoods. The CIP in this way differentiates itself from Vibrant Communities, the collective impact effort (funded by McConnell from 2002 to 2012) to reduce poverty within communities, although the two efforts share the goals of linking local constituencies, generating practical solutions to poverty, encouraging multisectoral collaboration, and beginning to create alignment around systemic change. Under the Vibrant Communities umbrella, a project in Saint-Michel, one of the lowest income neighbourhoods of Montreal, served as a model for the development of the neighbourhood roundtables that are now present across Montreal.

The CIP drew $23 million in commitments over six years from the nine foundations that agreed to participate. Centraide chose seventeen of the thirty existing neighbourhood roundtables, or "tables de quartier," in Montreal to receive support in the first phase. The pre-existence of these roundtables as community interest mediators has been critical to the design of the CIP. Each neighbourhood roundtable has been able to define local priorities for action which range across housing, food security, community infrastructure, and education, among others. Importantly, the foundations themselves do not direct their funding, leaving it to Centraide to ensure that flexible and adaptable funds are available to the individual communities to implement their action plans. In effect, the CIP was built on principles similar to trust-based philanthropy, requiring each foundation to trust the communities to determine their best course. According to a 2017 study[6] of the design of the CIP, the decision to bring in other funders from the beginning was in part to model this new, less-restricted form of funding. Centraide and the Chagnon Foundation, as co-architects, "believed that a broader funder collaborative could better impact systems-level outcomes by modelling new types of funding practices, and by influencing regional policy alignment in support of poverty reduction and community change."[7]

The CIP funders are not disengaged, although they are not involved in allocating the funds. One of the unusual aspects of the CIP is that the foundations themselves spend time regularly together, learning about comprehensive community change efforts, sharing information, and discussing outcomes. This time-demanding collaboration has not been without its challenges for individual foundations used to their own timeframes and decision-making. Recognizing the different interests of the nine foundations, the project governance model has shifted so they can participate with greater or lesser intensity, according to their preferences. Centraide has brokered relationships between funders and the participating communities, which has led in some cases to increased funding, in addition to that of the CIP, for opportunities as they arise within neighbourhoods. For example, the funders' familiarity with each other and their deeper relationships with the most vulnerable neighbourhoods of Montreal facilitated a rapid and successful effort during the pandemic by three of the nine CIP foundations to co-fund public health efforts in these hardest-hit communities. As CIP moves into a second phase of work and adopts a more regional focus, McConnell and the other CIP funders have developed a shared understanding of the drivers of poverty and social exclusion across the region of Montreal and are seeing the opportunities for systemic change at a regional level. The funder community in Montreal is small and relatively tight-knit, and the experience of the CIP, as well as other collaborative funding initiatives, have made it possible for more private funders to align their strategies and funding around a shared understanding of how to address systemic barriers. Local government partners have been at the CIP table from the beginning, which has also helped to align municipal plans for regional development with the learnings from the CIP work. As observers have concluded, "The CIP signals a shift in Montreal's funding landscape, in which philanthropy takes on an even greater role in setting the parameters and sculpting the contours of comprehensive community change work in Montreal. A shift of this nature has particular reverberations in Quebec where, in comparison with the rest of Canada, the state has continued to play a stronger role both in setting and delivering on social policy and in recognizing and supporting civil society and third-sector organizations."[8]

McConnell continues to focus and refine its commitment to Montreal since the arrival of a new president, Lili-Anna Pereša, in 2021. Pereša, the first francophone leader of McConnell, is intimately familiar with the Montreal community and with the CIP. She served as president of Centraide from 2012 to 2020 and sat at the CIP table from the beginning. Pereša and the board of McConnell, which comprises fourth and fifth generations of the McConnell family, have taken stock of the foundation's commitments and its role as a philanthropic leader in Montreal. By the end of 2021, McConnell had completed a strategic reflection and had tightened its focus as a national and local funder on three interconnected funding areas: community resilience, reconciliation, and climate change. While few of the current members of the board now live in Montreal, the McConnell family continues to feel a strong sense of attachment and obligation to the city. A portion of the funding and impact investments under each of its three strategic areas of focus will remain committed to organizations, projects, and communities in Montreal. And grants will continue to be made to support organizations working outside the focus areas that have a history with McConnell and have a positive impact on the greater Montreal community. The foundation is defining its criteria for this support to align it as much as possible with its overall strategic goals, while respecting the legacy of important relationships between McConnell and the place it has called home for over eighty years.

The Future of Place-based Philanthropy

Over the past five years, and particularly since the pandemic crisis, the disparities and inequalities among neighbourhoods in Canada's urban centres have been highlighted. Despite the many years of effort to reduce poverty and increase economic opportunity in Canada's cities, these disparities are clearer than ever. It is also clear that there is an intersection between racialized communities and economic and social inequality. Poverty in cities is found not only in neighbourhoods where there has been long-standing lack of access to education, housing, and jobs, but also disproportionately in neighbourhoods where racialized immigrants have settled and are struggling to move out of poverty. The future of place-based, neighbourhood-strengthening philanthropy hinges on the integration of a commitment to racial justice as well as social and economic justice. A foundation that is already actively engaged in this work is the Atkinson Foundation, led by Colette Murphy. Murphy began her career as a front-line refugee settlement worker before taking on three different management roles at the United Way Greater Toronto. She moved on to become a senior program director at the Metcalf Foundation responsible for the creation of its community program, and later its redesign and launch as a program focused on inclusive local economies. Murphy joined the Atkinson Foundation as its executive director in 2012.

Under Murphy's leadership, Atkinson turned its strategic focus from poverty reduction to poverty elimination while continuing to advocate for early childhood education, employment insurance, and other public policies related to social and economic justice. In 2014, the foundation's board of directors embarked on a decade of "movement strengthening" to grow the base of support in Ontario for public policies that create decent work and inclusive economic growth. According to Murphy, "the Atkinson Foundation's preoccupation with equitable economic development is about more than jobs and employment training [or] ... labour market research and policy development. It's about working alongside commun-ities to build income, build assets, and – critically – build agency and democratic power for those groups who continue to be severely harmed by traditional economic thinking and strategies."[9]

The Atkinson Foundation was created in 1942 by husband and wife team Joseph Atkinson and Elmina Elliott. Atkinson was the publisher and owner of the *Toronto Star*, Canada's largest newspaper, and both he and

Elmina were crusaders for social and economic justice. Atkinson believed in "humanity above all" – that the well-being of all people comes first among all considerations. The so-called Atkinson Principles continue to provide editorial direction to the Star and guide the Atkinson Foundation as a grantmaker, advocate, and investor. These principles are: a strong and united Canada, civic engagement, individual and civil liberties, the necessary role of government, and workers' rights. The foundation is registered as a private foundation, but it is not a family foundation. Only one Atkinson descendant is on the board of directors. The foundation maintains its historic link to the *Toronto Star* by including a representative of the newspaper on the board, but the board functions as an independent group of skilled governance leaders.

The Atkinson Foundation deploys many of the tools described by Dr Phillips in pursuing its mission: it helps shape narratives, promotes policy change, supports knowledge co-creation, and dissemination. It combines all its assets – grants, investments, and public voice – to this end. For example, Atkinson has supported the development of community benefits agreements with developers and cultivated a network of anchor institutions in Toronto and other cities in Ontario dedicated to crafting a social procurement strategy that emphasizes local purchasing, sustainability, and other shared priorities. Atkinson has collaborated with Metcalf to provide multi-year funding to two organizations,[10] the Ontario Employment Education and Research Centre and the ACORN Institute Canada, that put workers and residents at the centre of everything they do. It has partnered with the *Toronto Star* to ensure coverage of news that is relevant to workers' lives and livelihoods. It has also supported fellowships to raise public awareness of policy issues that affect "the realities of working people and their communities."[11] All these interventions are connected to its overarching goal of a fair economy. As Murphy explains, "We work with community organizers, policy innovators and investors to challenge income, wealth and democratic inequality. Our work has multiple layers. It's been about more than workforce development or community wealth benefits. It's about restructuring economies to build more equal communities. Together we aim to rewrite the rules of an economy that we think is unfair."[12] Increasingly, Atkinson is focusing with its partners on amplifying the voices of workers and residents as a way of strengthening community and making better public policy.

To do this, Atkinson and other place-based philanthropic funders are aware they must respect each community's leadership and wisdom. Murphy observes that Atkinson's strength comes from deep, long-term relationships in communities. The foundation is a multi-year funder and partner. It is important for her and her colleagues to grapple with what it means to be accountable to the organizations they fund. This highlights trust as a crucial element in place-based philanthropy. One of the challenges posed by the upheavals of the pandemic and the fight for justice in all its dimensions is how to build trust between funders and community members when the context, background, and power dynamics of the two are very different. Murphy says it is important to be explicit about the underlying systemic barriers to equitable community development. She observes that "the health crisis, the racial crisis, climate change, increasing inequality and the immorality of capitalism taken together reinforce implicitly the importance of a commitment to racial justice. We're making these intersections even more explicit in everything we do."[13] Fundamental to building trust is making this commitment transparent. As the observers of the CIP have noted, "The very legitimacy of place-based philanthropy's changemaking ambitions and capacity depends on its ability to be transparent about goals, strategies, underlying assumptions and expectations, as well as on a willingness to engage in an ongoing dialogue with other important stakeholders."[14] Since 2014, the Atkinson Foundation has been documenting its efforts to strengthen movements for decent work and a fair economy and it plans to make public over the next two years much more of what it's been doing and learning.

In recent years, foundation leaders' awareness of intersecting injustices has deepened. And many of those who suffer these injustices are calling on funders to "shift the power" with respect to how money is moved by grantmakers to grant recipients. In the next chapter, I describe the strategies of three foundations that are trying to do just this, to "shift the power," in part through the use of so-called "participatory" grantmaking approaches.

Shifting Power

*The Lucie et André Chagnon Foundation, the Laidlaw
Foundation, the Lyle S. Hallman Foundation*

Participatory funding … is a structural fix to the broken power dynamics
in traditional funding – a way to change philanthropy and impact
investing from closed, opaque and expert-driven to open, transparent and
community-driven.

Ben Wrobel and Meg Massey, *Letting Go*

André Chagnon is a well-known name in the two worlds of Quebec business and philanthropy. In the decades between 1964 and 2000, he deployed
his formidable entrepreneurial skills to create and build Groupe Videotron,
a successful company in the cable television and communications fields.
During this time, he also made personal philanthropic contributions of
money and time to the social challenges that compelled him most: the
barriers faced by individuals who lacked the opportunity to live up to their
potential because of disability, addiction, lack of education, or other factors
stemming from poverty and inequality. After the sale of his company in
2000, Chagnon and his family decided to bring their entrepreneurial
approach and their ambitious vision of social good to the enterprise of
philanthropy. They were extraordinarily generous in pursuing this goal.
The family's private foundation, named after the founder and his wife,
Lucie, was endowed in 2000 with a gift of $1.4 billion, an unprecedented
amount at the time, which immediately made the foundation one of
the largest by assets in the country. Its vision was both aspirational and
consistent with the theme that had compelled André Chagnon in his
earliest philanthropic efforts: "To prevent poverty by helping to create
conditions that will enable all young people living in Quebec to develop
their full potential, particularly through educational success." Indeed,
"prevention" became the one-word motto of the Chagnon Foundation,
displayed on the entrance wall to the foundation's Montreal offices.

Despite its size, the Chagnon Foundation is not a pan-Canadian foundation. Its roots and its focus remain firmly in Quebec. Yet its ambition is sweeping. It wants to address the root causes of poverty, not just the symptoms. Its philosophy is preventive rather than ameliorative, stopping poverty before it becomes entrenched. This is an approach that other foundations fighting poverty have adopted, as we have seen in the preceding chapters. In its first fifteen years, however, the Chagnon Foundation ran into great and very public criticism from the communities it was trying to serve, which forced it to completely rethink its strategy.

What happened? The foundation made a big and ambitious bet by partnering directly with the government of Quebec in a large-scale effort to distribute funds in communities across Quebec through three jointly managed organizations delivering programs in support of healthy, active lifestyles, early child development, and student retention in schools. These were the elements of a prevention strategy aimed at helping young people grow out of poverty and into healthy and successful adult lives. The partnership with the government was appealing because it promised a way to scale the effort quickly across many regions of the province. But it ran into opposition from many of the intended local recipients and partners who saw it as an undemocratic imposition on communities of the foundation's own priorities and preferences, and a perceived distortion of public priorities by a private philanthropist. As it faced this opposition, the foundation went through a learning experience that has radically shifted its approach from an entrepreneurial mode of building enterprises to a collaborative and participatory mode of network strengthening. Chagnon has been one of the rare private foundations that has done its learning in the public eye, reflecting on its experience, and sharing its lessons quite openly. The learning has translated into an ongoing commitment by the foundation to listen more closely to communities, very much in line with the tenets of modern participatory grantmaking.

Participatory Grantmaking

It's a very different world today than twenty years ago. In many ways, it's a world in which decisions, views, and actions are more widely shared, largely by digital means. The democratization of opinion has shaped the attitudes of younger generations and forced older generations to become more aware. As social movement builders Henry Timms and Jeremy Heimans noted in their book *New Power*, "Thanks to today's ubiquitous connectivity, we can come together and organize ourselves in ways that are geographically boundless and highly distributed and with unprecedented velocity and reach. This hyperconnectedness has given birth to new models and mindsets that are shaping our age."[1] Digital technologies have forced all sectors of business, from retail to transportation to media and communications, to accelerate and to connect. These technologies have changed the operations of organizations in the non-profit sector too. Charities are using digital tools and platforms for communications, fundraising, and collaboration. The crisis of the pandemic itself has led to more acquisition and use of digital tools as internal operations were forced online. Of course, the act of adding digital tools and technologies does not automatically lead to more open or transparent systems. But these tools offer possibilities for a different and wider engagement and participation of employees, clients, and partners. Non-profit organizations are taking advantage of them to reach new donors, get better client feedback, look for new partners, and interact with others more than ever before.

How are these developments and expectations touching the world of foundations? For some years, people have wondered when or if there was going to be a shakeup in the typical practices of the grantmaking foundation, run behind closed doors, at its own pace, with funding decisions made by a small and non-diverse group. The world-shaking influence of the pandemic does seem to have broken long-standing assumptions and behaviours in grantmaking philanthropy. Is this a permanent change? To be frank, most foundations are not known for moving quickly. The practices of institutional grantmaking have been remarkably slow to change. The digital revolution has stopped at the door of many foundations. It is not unusual, for example, for foundations to ignore or decline to invest in digital tools that permit more effective grants data collection and sharing, while charities eagerly seek to invest in digital platforms to manage their fundraising and client services. Many, if not most, foundations still practise a model of granting that is held internally, with timelines and decisions made by their boards and conditions set and imposed on grantees rather than developed in collaboration with them. This is a model that has created many frustrations for those outside of it. As Ben Soskis, a historian and critic of foundations has noted, "The generally slow pace of foundation grantmaking is regarded by many … as strategically ineffective and grossly insensitive, a sort of paternalism that imposes funders' time frames on grantees."[2] The pandemic broke this model, at least temporarily, for many funders as they lifted grant restrictions and conditions, agreed to provide general operating support, and disbursed with much greater urgency. Their actions lent credibility to the idea that they were prepared to let go of some of the power they had not been willing to share before. Soskis comments that during the pandemic, "Norms promoting recipients' agency have been strengthened by another related set prioritizing speed, urgency and the need to check a donor-centric orientation."[3] The calls are growing louder for funders to continue to "shift the power" to grantees, and to begin to do this with an eye to shifting power specifically to the least powerful, to those marginalized and racialized groups that have not received much funding previously from philanthropic foundations.

In this context, funders and charities are paying more attention to an approach called "participatory grantmaking." As the term suggests, this is about increasing participation by people with lived experience in the decision-making about the allocation of funds to solve social problems. It can range from consulting or being advised by people who may be affected by the grant, to giving over the decision-making power entirely to communities that will receive the funds. While it has been documented as a practice over the last decade, particularly in the United States, it is still far from being in the mainstream. There are many perceived obstacles to its adoption. Some foundations are following strategies that do not easily lend themselves to participatory processes. They may be highly focused on research or on a smaller number of institutional grantees, such as universities, or on their own operations. They may not be community or place-based and not familiar with local or grassroots community organizations. Some foundations are concerned about sharing decision-making for the sake of fiduciary accountability or legal reasons, or because they fear conflict of interest. Many in Canada have few staff and do not have internal capacity to manage a more participatory approach.[4] Despite funder reluctance, I don't believe these are obstacles that should prevent funders of any type from considering the question of how they use their power and how they might share it. In this more open age of "new power," it may not even be a choice.

A 2021 book on the developing practice of participatory funding by American authors Ben Wrobel and Meg Massey sets out a clear framework for foundations that might want to consider how to shift their decision-making power at key steps in the funding process. They note that most funders design their processes around three decisions points:

developing a theory of change, or a hypothesis about what problem they want to solve; building a pipeline of ideas about how to solve that problem; and deciding whom to fund. In their view, "every one of these decision points offers an opportunity for grantmakers to engage people outside of their organizations."[5] There are multiple techniques for creating participatory processes at each of these decision points, from inviting community members to identify priority challenges to creating open calls for proposals. Funders can establish external advisory committees or decision-making bodies that make decisions on proposals for board approval. Funders can also simply allocate funds to external pooled or collaborative funds managed by community members. Wrobel and Massey reference another framework for measuring participation that can be usefully applied by funders to their thinking about participatory processes. This is the "ladder of citizen participation"[6] developed in the 1960s by American planner Sherry Arnstein to illustrate visually how decision-makers can engage community members in any civic process. The eight-rung ladder's lowest two rungs are grouped as "nonparticipation." The next set of three rungs are grouped as "tokenism." The highest set of three rungs are grouped as "citizen control." The key to designing participatory approaches is to consider to what degree citizens, communities, and grantees are being given actual control over decisions at various points in the stages of funding. Not all stages may offer or lend themselves to participation at the highest rung of the ladder. But Wrobel and Massey suggest that participatory grantmakers keep in mind that this sort of decision-making is a journey, not a destination, with several key principles: "Involve the people most affected by the issues in decision-making about addressing them. Go beyond just listening and make sure you engage, rather than inform. Be transparent. Remember that there is a role for experts and professionals, as partners and facilitators. And finally, remember that any participatory process should be in a constant state of iteration and self-reflection."[7]

In this chapter I explore approaches and examples of this more participatory approach to philanthropy by telling the stories of three foundations, all of which work with youth and families. The Lucie et André Chagnon Foundation, one of the largest family foundations in Canada, launched an unprecedented listening tour across Quebec to invite citizens to help shape its new strategic approach of supporting community mobilization and building networks to change systems. The Laidlaw Foundation in Toronto, a foundation focused on at-risk youth, added young directors to its board and youth representatives to its granting advisory committees to ensure their voices were heard in grant decision-making. The Lyle S. Hallman Foundation in Kitchener-Waterloo adopted a collaborative approach to its place-based grantmaking, including youth and volunteers in a donations advisory committee and working closely with its grantees throughout the funding relationship.

The Lucie et André Chagnon Foundation

In an article in 2017, Jean-Marc Chouinard, the president of the Chagnon Foundation, summed up the critical messages received from the communities in which the foundation was working: "Don't tell us, support us;" "don't negotiate, collaborate;" "don't replace government, complement it;" and "don't monitor, learn."[8] Faced with this criticism, Chouinard described the reverse course of the foundation in the 2015–17 period. It came from a dawning realization that they were taking a wrong turn, that the strategy they were using had become transactional not relational, and that the foundation risked losing its legitimacy as an actor in a larger social ecosystem. The partnership with the government was not renewed in 2015. The foundation embarked on a period of self-questioning, aided by a team of external academic observers who had been working with the foundation since 2010 as developmental evaluators. The key initiative the foundation undertook in this period was to go out into the communities across Quebec and to engage people in conversation about what they thought was needed to tackle the enormous challenge of giving young people a better start to their lives. This wasn't a small undertaking. Over the course of a little more than a year, foundation staff held sixty-eight meetings with over 760 people drawn from many different contexts: the community itself, municipal governments, early childhood, education and public health organizations, universities, unions, and other social sector players. Chouinard noted that "this proved to be a significant step towards our regaining a certain degree of legitimacy."[9] As he tells the story, this consultation exercise was built on a base of renewed trust from community organizations that began with informal contacts with local organizations. The foundation staff were careful to stay in listening mode during these informal sessions. Chouinard describes it as being in a mode of mutual learning rather than in a mode of evaluation and criticism.[10] In effect, the foundation wanted to have a continuing dialogue with the community in which all could share what they were learning and what was needed to advance toward mutually desired goals of preventing poverty and giving all young people in Quebec the chance to succeed through education.

What the foundation learned, as it moved toward a strategy built on reinforcing productive relationships with community players, was that instead of funding newly created individual organizations, as in the partnership with government, it could provide greater value by acting as a long-term funder for organizations and networks that help to mobilize collective action in communities. This role is consistent with the core idea of participatory funding, which is shifting the decision-making power into more hands. The foundation has slowly transformed itself since 2013 into a self-described network weaver under the guidance of local communities. Chagnon now partners with community-driven and community-based networks of all kinds in Quebec to help them act collectively, develop their skills, evaluate themselves better, and communicate and influence others more effectively. Chagnon also supports intermediaries that share learning resources, data, and practices, and work to build public awareness. Chouinard is clear that Chagnon's role is "not to come up with solutions to be implemented by others but to support those who are on a journey to innovate, seek and implement their own solutions."[11] It is one of many players in an ecosystem, not an actor but a builder of infrastructure that supports other actors.

Chouinard is also clear that to have the greatest impact the foundation's own leaders and people must share aligned values and behaviours. Chagnon's engagement as a participatory funder implies that it must make itself accessible and clear about what it is doing and how it is acting on the input of its partners. The foundation has engaged in a process of deliberate internal transformation, focusing systematically on how to make all its processes and systems coherent with the needs and priorities of communities. The pandemic accelerated this work of internal re-alignment of its structures and processes, from governance to financial systems, to human resources to communications. At the same time, the pandemic has added urgency to the internal aspiration for change. Chouinard, himself a former Olympic athlete, quotes a phrase, "Pressure is a privilege," used by leading sports figures such as Doc Rivers, the coach of the Boston Celtics and Billie Jean King, the tennis player. Under the pressure of community expectations and pandemic urgency, the foundation, he says, has a privileged opportunity to work even harder to change from inside. Chouinard confirms that the foundation is continuing to listen to its partners and to reach out to those communities where it has not been listening before, particularly to Black and Indigenous communities. In the summer of 2021, it conducted another survey of its community partners to get their opinions on its efforts to build more trusting relationships characterized by responsiveness and relevance to community needs. The results were impressive. Virtually all the respondents reported a favourable opinion of the foundation and 84 per cent said they felt "close" to the organization.[12] This is a remarkable turnaround from 2015. And in the phase of community recovery from the pandemic, the foundation, according to Chouinard, intends to continue its efforts to align its behaviours and systems with its organizational values of solidarity, social justice, inclusion, collaboration, and agility.

The Laidlaw Foundation

The vision of the Chagnon Foundation in Quebec for a society in which youth can reach their full potential finds an echo in the vision of a much older private foundation in Toronto, the Laidlaw Foundation. This foundation was created in 1949 by two brothers, Robert and Walter Laidlaw, and Robert's sons, Rod and Nick. The foundation funded a typical mix of charitable causes for the times: the arts, neighbourhood social services, and health facilities. It was also an early investor in protecting the natural environment. Fairly quickly, Laidlaw developed an interest in addressing local conditions of poverty in the rapidly growing city of Toronto. Under the leadership of the first two generations of Laidlaws, the foundation began contributing at a Canada-wide level, not only as a funder of services to alleviate local poverty, but also as a funder of ideas about the role of government and the development of a welfare state. Influenced by the expertise of staff leaders with backgrounds in social work, the foundation began to focus on the challenges facing children at risk. Over three or four decades, Laidlaw became one of the most active private funders supporting youth at risk, with a mix of strategies that included funds for research and policy development as well as direct services. From the earliest stages, the Laidlaws were unusually willing to share their philanthropic work with professional staff and advisers. Indeed, the foundation's board has not been dominated by family members since the 1980s. The foundation's first external expert advisory committees for grants were created in 1963. As the foundation became more tightly focused in the 1990s on children and youth at risk, under the leadership of its executive director, Nathan Gilbert, it supported Canada-wide policy development and advocacy efforts to lift children out of poverty and continued to work with experts in child development and social welfare policies.

A shift toward greater participation from young people themselves began in the first decade of the 2000s, as Laidlaw built on its long-standing values around social justice with a newly stated commitment to inclusion, diversity, and civic and youth engagement. Gilbert had a deep personal conviction about the importance of listening to youth directly. The foundation translated this into funding youth to engage with the foundation in shaping its programming efforts. The key structural and strategic shift toward participatory funding and power-sharing, however, took place after the arrival of a new executive director, Jehad Aliweiwi, in 2014. Aliweiwi came with grassroots experience in managing community services in diverse neighbourhoods as the former executive director of the Thorncliffe Neighbourhood Office in downtown Toronto. He had a heightened understanding of the multiple challenges faced by young people from immigrant, lower-income, and diverse ethnic communities because of his work with families, many of whom were immigrants from South Asia and the Middle East. With his direction, Laidlaw began to focus specifically on youth at risk, in care, or in the justice system. The foundation still had the mix of strategies it had followed for years under the leadership of Gilbert: granting, convening, research, and advocacy. But Aliweiwi and his board of directors understood, just as Chouinard and his board did at the Chagnon Foundation, that to adopt a truly participatory approach, they needed to evolve their staff, structures, and systems both internally and externally. It wasn't enough to fund youth engagement activities or convene youth to identify opportunities for themselves. There had to be consistency across the foundation in terms of its own behaviours. In words that echo those of Chouinard at Chagnon, Aliweiwi says "The foundation needs to be mindful of coherence between its values, skills and behaviours. [We need to consider] the lenses we use, and how varied experiences are brought to bear. Our values and practices need to be aligned."[13] Shared values of the foundation, such as engagement and empowerment, responsiveness and equity, are shaping the practices of a more participatory approach at Laidlaw, just as they are at Chagnon.

Organizational change in a foundation takes time. But after seven or eight years, it is more than evident at Laidlaw. The Laidlaw board is highly diverse, with over two-thirds of its directors drawn from the racialized communities of Toronto, including Black and Indigenous populations. Aliweiwi suggests the Laidlaw board is setting the standard "by a mile" for its composition. Its president is an Indigenous woman, Janine Manning. Many directors are younger, to reflect the primary population Laidlaw serves. Their perspectives are shaping bold funding decisions, such as a 2021 gift of $2.5 million to an endowment for a new Foundation for Black Communities, which a young Laidlaw board member, Rebecca Darwent, helped to launch in collaboration with another former Laidlaw board member, Liban Abokor. In Aliweiwi's view, "Strong representation on the board from Black and Indigenous communities is very effective ... these directors are from the communities or know them ... their decision-making is a powerful reflection of these communities."[14] Similarly, the staff at Laidlaw are drawn from diverse racial backgrounds and have lived experience in communities. They were recruited for their experience and skills in doing hands-on work with the grantee organizations, many of which have young leaders who benefit from leadership coaching and support. The staff also work with advisory committees that continue to play an important role for Laidlaw, not only for subject expertise but also because they provide a means to bring community voices and needs directly to the decision-making table. For example, Laidlaw has an Indigenous Advisory Committee to guide its Indigenous Strategy. Eight young Indigenous leaders helped Laidlaw develop an Indigenous Youth and Community Futures Fund and ensured that the activities supported by Laidlaw's grants are "reflective of Indigenous youth priorities with a focus on land, language and culture" and "the application and selection processes are more accessible and equitable for youth."[15] Laidlaw has also taken advantage of opportunities to participate financially in collective funds, such as the Indigenous Peoples Resilience Fund and the Foundation for Black Communities, which are led by members of the communities they are intended to benefit.

While the granting process at Laidlaw is highly participatory, this does not mean decision-making shifts entirely to the community. The foundation has not stepped back from suggesting (and funding) specific initiatives designed to build the operational capacity of many of its grantees. Its Youth Action Fund and Youth Collective Impact initiative

support grassroots projects led by and for youth who are underserved by
education and overrepresented in the justice and child welfare systems.
Aliweiwi notes that these youth have great need for management training.
"Embedded in our funding strategy," he says, "is support for the capacity
of an organization to manage itself. Passionate young people are not always
so good at implementing their ideas. We are upfront with our board
that investing in grassroots organizations is very risky. Capacity building
is an intentional addition to every grant. We are clear that we are here
to support them to do what they do well while maintaining accountability and good management."[16] This is an example of the dance that
grantmaking foundations with a participatory approach often perform,
between their wish to give power into the hands of community and
their need to maintain boundaries on the amount of risk they accept.
Aliweiwi feels his board has become more flexible and more open to risk
as Laidlaw has continued to focus more deeply on the complex challenges
facing marginalized youth. The pace of change and the responsiveness
of his board and staff team have been even more pronounced since the
pandemic in a way that has surprised and pleased him. It was "hard to
predict," he says, "that Laidlaw would have evolved as it has ... I would
not have predicted it even ten years ago." Yet what is clear is that the
strong commitment to social justice evident in the actions of the Laidlaw
founders were enough to set the foundation on the road to its current
role as a strong participatory funder.

The Lyle S. Hallman Foundation

Like the Chagnon Foundation in Quebec and the Laidlaw Foundation in
Toronto, the Lyle S. Hallman Foundation, based in Waterloo, Ontario,
has a purpose centred on the well-being and potential of young people.
The Hallman and Chagnon foundations were created virtually at the same
time in the early 2000s, both by successful businessmen, and both very
much regionally based. The two foundations have a similar philosophy
around the importance of prevention, or upstream intervention, before
problems occur, rather than dealing with the consequences downstream.
The Hallman Foundation focuses on young people and their families,
and the neighbourhoods, institutions, and systems that serve and connect
them. It was set up in 2003 as a public foundation, not a private foundation. Its founder, Lyle Shantz Hallman, did not intend to establish a family

philanthropy but rather to create a long-term independent philanthropic institution (although Hallman's son James is on the board of directors). Hallman was a very successful builder and developer in the Waterloo Region who had been a generous individual donor to local hospitals and universities before starting the foundation. He set his stamp on the goals of the foundation from the outset by directing support to local institutions and programs that made a difference in the lives of children, especially those from low-income families. Hallman died unexpectedly, in 2003, just after creating his foundation, leaving it to the board to develop its approach and funding focus. Even though Hallman is not present to build his philanthropic legacy, Laura Manning, the foundation's executive director, confirms that "Lyle's legacy does shape the choice of priorities. The board discusses what his intentions were and how much they should be bound by them."[17]

While Hallman did not envision how sizeable his namesake foundation would become, it is now a dominant philanthropic player in the Waterloo region, granting about $15 million a year. With this size comes a certain social and moral obligation to community, Manning acknowledges. It took some time for the board and staff to settle on a set of values and guiding principles, but their approach is now clearly and publicly articulated: "We believe strongly in engaged philanthropy. To us, this means maintaining a close and active relationship with grantees over an extended period and contributing more than just funds. We may help an organization connect with the right expertise; we may advocate on their behalf to government or other stakeholders. Underpinning this concept is the creation of a safe and frank relationship where both parties are open to honest dialogue and problem solving."[18] As in the case of Chagnon and Laidlaw, Hallman is working to align its systems, staff, and processes with the commitment to transparency and frankness that is explicit in its mission statement and values. For some years, Hallman has worked with a donations advisory committee of community members who advise the executive director in sorting grant applications for board approval by reviewing and providing their own expertise and community knowledge to the choice of applications. More recently, Hallman also uses external reviewers on the applications, chosen for their subject matter expertise or because of their depth of understanding of the community. This is a useful channel for bringing more diversity of opinion to the table and to the assessments made by the staff and advisory committee.

It's also one being adopted by more foundations as they respond to the pressure for more interaction with communities and less secretiveness in their granting. But it does not yet represent moving to the highest rungs of the Arnstein ladder of citizen participation, even for a foundation such as Hallman that is very connected to its local community. More recently, Hallman has decided to "walk the talk" on its commitment to youth engagement by asking youth themselves, aged from fourteen to twenty-four, to get involved in reviewing grant applications, particularly for projects directly involving youth. "It's been challenging but in the last six months (of 2020) we have got it more nailed down," says Manning. "We are working with existing partners such as the YWCA and neighbourhood associations to find the youth [reviewers]. Their input gets rolled into the process with the same weight as that of our experts and the donations advisory committee."[19]

In 2018, Hallman took significant steps along the participatory funding road. It decided to pilot what it called Neighbourhood Action Grants, small grants of up to $500 made to residents to help them act on things they care about in their communities. This program was co-designed with the communities themselves through local community centres. Structured as a pilot in 2018, it expanded from two to four neighbourhoods in 2019, and will continue after a pandemic-caused slowdown. From the outset, the goal was to make this a participatory exercise, with neighbourhood residents engaged in working on the development of ideas for projects and taking the lead in implementing them. The projects were small in scale and as straightforward as craft activities, yard sales, bazaars, and potlucks. But in each case the goal was to help neighbours make connections, build relationships, develop project leadership skills, and engage youth. Hallman's motivation for this move toward greater participation by people in designing and managing project grants was its interest in building the capacity of communities for making their own change. "Social change happens either at hyper-local levels or at high systemic levels," notes Manning. "We were working in the middle but not shifting anything. The board looked intentionally at more strategies to get involved at grassroots levels."[20] She acknowledges this is labour-intensive work both for the coaches and community centre staff involved in working with the residents, and for the foundation staff. It required significant support from a foundation staff person with her own experience in community development and coaching expertise to act as a liaison and support to all the communities. This certainly poses a challenge for expansion beyond the four neighbourhoods in which the program operates. But the pilot has clearly met its goals, even with the pandemic interruption. Hallman has commissioned developmental evaluations along the way, which it has published on its website to share its learnings with others.

In another experiment to build the capacity of organizations and collaboratives in communities to work on social change, Hallman launched a pilot in 2018 to provide general operating support (GOS) funds without restrictions to organizations wanting to invest in their core functions, such as human resources, technology, marketing, fundraising, and evaluation. This type of funding shifts control and power to the recipient organizations to determine how best to invest in their own capacities, rather than answering to foundation specifications. Hallman funded developmental evaluations of this initiative as well, publishing reports on its website so that others could learn from Hallman's experience. When the pandemic struck in 2020, the foundation already had two years of experience with the GOS pilot which gave it confidence to make changes in its broader granting portfolio and to quickly lift restrictions and proactively offer grants with more confidence and trust in its community partners. These partners confirmed that this contributed significantly to their stability and capacity to meet community needs. As the pandemic ebbs, the foundation is considering how to make some of its changes in granting practice more permanent. Manning concedes that this type of trust-based, unconditional funding is not yet a norm in philanthropy. "If all you do is relax [conditions] it's easy to contract back again," she notes. "Has practice really shifted? It's a good start ... but systems tend to revert to their stasis point."[21] Nevertheless, the Hallman Foundation demonstrated during the pandemic that it had learned already to share more power through its granting practices. A study of Hallman's approach during the crisis concluded that "one of the things that enabled the Foundation to move quickly and pursue the actions it took was that it has already established a culture and way of working that valued trust and communication. Things like unrestricted granting and trust-based philanthropy were not new concepts for them, and there was already a degree of comfort at both the staff and Board level toward sharing power and taking more risks with its granting and reporting requirements."[22]

Conclusion

The stories of these foundations demonstrate the essential observation on participatory funding made by Wrobel and Massey: the process is the point. It's not so much about the end or the outcome but more about the way in which a funder goes about building different and more participatory processes with its partners and actively learning as it goes. All three foundations describe themselves as being in a constant iterative state of learning about their interactions with fund recipients and with the wider group of beneficiaries in the community. It will take some time. Foundations will continue to use constraints around staff, internal capacity, time, accountability, and donor restrictions to explain why they are not considering more participatory redesign of their processes. But these three examples may be evidence of a change that will come more quickly than we expect to the traditional models and processes of institutional philanthropy. Long-time observers of foundation practices have been surprised by the rapidity of the responses to the pandemic crisis. Julia Coffman of the Center for Evaluation Innovation has studied the loosening of restrictions and power-sharing models of several Canadian and American foundations, including Hallman, during the pandemic. She concludes, "We don't know yet whether foundations will treat this period as a temporary departure from business-as-usual, or whether they will see it as the beginning of a new normal. My hope is for the latter, and that more democratic ways of learning ultimately align with more democratic ways of developing strategy, working with partners, and engaging generally in the complex work of social change."[23]

Advancing Public Policy

Maytree, Max Bell Foundation, the Muttart Foundation

Good public policy improves the lives of Canadians, and contributions from charities can significantly improve the public policy that governments make.

Allan Northcott, president, Max Bell Foundation

The Maytree Foundation is not a typical private foundation, nor does it describe itself that way. Known publicly and simply as Maytree, it is a charity with an activist philosophy. Its mission is to advance systemic solutions to poverty and to strengthen civic communities through a human rights approach. Maytree sees itself as a changemaker, using grants as its tools. At the same time, it runs its own programs and operations and has a permanent staff of fourteen, which is larger than usual for a family foundation in Canada. Forty years ago, in 1982, when its founders Alan and Judy Broadbent registered Maytree as a private foundation, it was recognizably a family philanthropic vehicle, although it was never an endowed fund. Today, Broadbent and his wife are still the principal funders of the organization, providing funds annually to support an operating and grantmaking budget. The couple and their two sons form the majority of the five-member board of directors. According to Elizabeth McIsaac, president of Maytree, Alan Broadbent continues to be actively involved in the goals and strategies of Maytree, working in partnership with her and her staff, and keeping an office on-site that he visits almost daily. He is one of the rare philanthropic leaders in Canada who takes an active public speaking and writing role, producing editorials, blogs, and speeches that are published and circulated through Maytree's website.

Alan Broadbent is personally interested in the systems and policy frameworks that shape the urban experience. He has an enduring interest in contributing to policy development through "ideas that matter," to borrow the name of an organization he founded in 1997 that promotes public debate on "issues relevant to cities and the values of diversity, community and the public good."[1] His thinking is shaped by his continuing questions and conversations with a wide network of peers and colleagues. Broadbent has not hesitated to use philanthropic funding to create new platforms and structures beyond Maytree itself to shape the policy conversation. In 1992, for example, Broadbent and social policy researcher Ken Battle launched the Caledon Institute of Social Policy, which, over the next twenty-five years, with core financial support from Broadbent and Maytree, became an influential source of policy ideas around income security, work, housing, and care, the essential elements that need to be in place for people to lift themselves and their families from poverty.

In engaging in policy development, Broadbent is far from the norm as a philanthropist. Consistent with being "under the radar," most private foundations in Canada don't participate in developing or advocating for public policy change. This reluctance to engage extends even to funding charities that are active in policy work. It has roots in an aversion to being "out in front" or to drawing public attention for advocacy efforts. In part it's also due to a lack of staff expertise. Foundations, like many charities, believe policy work is not a legitimate charitable activity because it is "political" and Canadian regulators do not permit it, although this is not the case. Fundamentally, many private foundations in Canada are uneasy with the idea of intervening in the public space that is dominated by government. Deference to government's role in determining policy priorities is characteristic of Canadian philanthropy. Most private foundations avoid the issue by framing their purpose and work around amelioration rather than prevention of problems. On complex social and economic challenges, such as poverty, a foundation will focus more on funding the supply of services to people in poverty than on changing the demand or need for those services. Nonetheless, thinking through public policy change is important even from an ameliorative perspective. At a local level, for example, low-income people's access to services is affected by public policy decisions in the areas of transportation, housing, education, parks, and public spaces. Public policy decisions provide context to our physical and built environment, our economic opportunities, our community supports, and our social and cultural interactions. We know that public policy matters. Arguably, for any private foundation, it's a necessary question to ponder: "Why *not* engage with public policy on the issues and communities that matter to us?"

I would make three arguments – moral, strategic, and structural – for more philanthropic engagement with public policy. From a moral standpoint, a foundation should consider its obligation to serve the public good. In 2016, Dr Roger Gibbins, then a senior fellow of Max Bell Foundation, put it this way in a lengthy paper written for Max Bell: "Charitable status and the financial benefits it conveys create a moral imperative to pursue the public good and to be engaged as policy advocates in political and ethical debates about policy and social change."[2] In his view, the privilege conferred by a charitable designation carries with it a responsibility to contribute a moral perspective on the creation of public policy, including equity, justice, and a democratic diversity of voices in the process. I would add that foundations, as organizations with a long life, have a moral obligation to think and speak for the benefit of future generations and the public good of our society, not just today, but in times beyond the horizon. In this sense, foundations could and should engage in public policy work as a public benefit to the future. Foundations working on climate change and environmental policy, for example, see themselves as acting on a moral obligation to those not yet born.

From a strategic perspective, foundations that want to have impact in their work with community partners can see that public policies affect the prospects for success or failure in almost any program intended to serve the community and/or specific clients. To take an example, successfully supporting youth at risk through mentoring and coaching after school depends on public policies that fund community spaces, create parks and recreation facilities, ensure supportive and flexible policing and a fair justice system, to name a few conditions. These policies are determined by elected officials who listen to community advocates. Even if a foundation is not engaging in policy advocacy, it can make room in its granting for funds to support such advocacy by the charities most directly involved in delivering the services. Without policy advocacy, these charities are putting their fingers in one small hole of a leaking dike. It is almost unavoidable that they should raise their voices with public policy makers. As Gibbins vividly puts it, for these charities, "picking up the government cheque for service delivery creates an obligation to also pick up the policy sword."[3]

From a structural perspective, foundations have advantages and opportunities to play roles in policy debates that are not available to others in the charitable sector. They can play an indirect role behind the scenes as arms-length funders of university or think tank policy research, or as conveners of policy debates among multiple players. They can commission and circulate contributions to policy discussions at different levels of government. They can build policy capacity directly within charities through training, or at a sector level by funding policy staff positions in umbrella associations or in collective movements and networks. More directly, they can raise their own voices, either individually or together, to influence policy debates. While rare, we see more instances of this direct action by foundations in recent years. For example, the Early Childhood Development Funders Working Group (ECDFWG), made up of eight different private and public foundations, has issued three open letters since 2015 urging policy and government investments in early childhood learning and care. The Lucie et André Chagnon Foundation in Quebec, in addition to joining the ECDFWG advocacy efforts, has made numerous submissions to Quebec parliamentary commissions on issues related to poverty, the rights of children and youth, child development, and education. Several Quebec-based anglophone and francophone foundations, including Chagnon, McConnell, Saputo, Trottier, Béati, Dufresne et Gauthier and others have come together to sign open letters to public policy makers on subjects such as economic inequality, the need for social housing, and the impact of systemic racism.[4]

In summary, foundations can play multiple roles in policy work by virtue of their structural and functional flexibility. The range of options for incorporating public policy approaches into their portfolios, coupled with considerations of strategic impact and moral obligation, make a strong case for engaging in public policy. Private funders can add unique value to the policy work of charities and to the development of policy ideas for government. Despite this, the number of private foundations in Canada doing such work remains surprisingly small. For the reasons stated earlier, most foundations do not feel confident or do not feel it is appropriate for them to do so. Growing public suspicion of the influence of private foundations over the last several years is making it more difficult, rather than easier, for Canadian foundations to fund the work and defend their legitimacy to do so at the same time.

In this context, models matter very much. Some Canadian foundations have been leaders in this field for years. Their founders and directors have had direct experience with the public sphere, for example Walter Gordon, former politician and Cabinet minister who created The Walter and Duncan Gordon Foundation (now known simply as The Gordon Foundation) dedicated to improving Canadian public policy, particularly in the areas of water and Northern development.[5] Or foundation donors and staff leaders, such as Alan Broadbent and Elizabeth McIsaac of Maytree, who have a deep interest in policy ideas and frameworks that shape the outcomes of the work of their community partners. In the following pages, I focus on three private foundations, each of which has been an innovative funder with a significant impact on policy development with and for the charitable sector in Canada. Maytree in Toronto has funded original research and policy development, fostered policy debates, and developed a first-of-its kind policy training program for charities. Its work on policy training also served as a model for Max Bell Foundation of Calgary, which supports innovations in public policy and practices in the areas of health, education, and the environment. The Muttart Foundation of Edmonton is one of the few private foundations in Canada that has committed itself to a sustained effort to improve the federal regulatory policy environment for all registered charities. There are other important private funders in Canada, such as the McConnell, Metcalf, Gordon, Lawson, Atkinson, Ivey, and Chagnon foundations, which play an influential role in public policy in Canada. The three profiled in this chapter have made public policy development a central and public part of their mission and purpose.

Maytree

From its beginnings in the 1980s, Maytree focused on poverty in the Toronto area where Alan Broadbent and his family are based. The first three decades of Maytree's work were closely identified with the exploration of the barriers facing newer immigrants to Toronto, many of whom were coming from Asia, the Caribbean, and Africa, and struggling to move out of the poverty in which they found themselves on their arrival in Toronto. Starting with support for adult literacy programs, Maytree moved into supporting immigrants and refugees with an increasingly broad range of initiatives, from access to education through mentoring and scholarships to labour market entry through skills qualification and networking. Influencing public policy was a goal from the outset.

Broadbent and his staff at Maytree saw public policy engagement as a strategy to help overcome the systemic barriers facing immigrants emerging from poverty in an urban setting. Elizabeth McIsaac comments that Maytree has looked for "levers that shift systems and policies in a bigger way. ... [For Maytree] public policy change is that lever."[6] By 2005, Maytree's public policy work on supporting immigrants and refugees was recognized with the Paul Ylvisaker Award for Public Policy Engagement from the US Council on Foundations. Maytree was cited for its efforts to change immigration policies in Canada through public awareness campaigns and other activities, for work that resulted in a policy that allows refugees without permanent-resident status to receive loans for post-secondary education, and for the creation, in 2003, of the Toronto Region Immigrant Employment Council[7], a multisectoral effort to generate solutions to the issue of immigrant un- and under-employment. In 2005, Broadbent and his colleagues, acting on the realization that few community organization leaders had direct experience in policy development and advocacy, decided to start the innovative Public Policy Training Institute as an effort to strengthen the capacity of civil society organizations and leaders to engage with public policy. Now called the Maytree Policy School, and offered as a six-month program, it is focused on professionals working in non-profits focusing on social policy with the goal of helping them learn how to advance evidence-based policy solutions.

By 2015, Broadbent and his Maytree colleagues had evolved further in their approach to tackling the roots of urban poverty. They decided to shift to a human rights approach, reasoning, as McIsaac put it, that poverty can be defined as the absence of social and economic rights being fulfilled. Public policy work was still very much in the forefront of this approach. Maytree seized an opportunity to engage in the development of a National Housing Strategy, which the federal government was exploring after 2015. Maytree, working with thought leaders in the housing field, identified the need to recognize housing as a human right in the National Housing Strategy, knowing that many Canadians live in conditions of housing poverty. It joined with other civil society leaders in a four-year public advocacy campaign for housing as a human right that culminated in the adoption by Parliament in 2019 of the *National Housing Strategy Act*.

Maytree continues to focus on the evolution of human rights-based frameworks and structures at the local level with advocacy work on human rights cities – cities that base some of their policies on international human rights principles in areas such as employment, social security, access to housing, food security, water, education, health, and an adequate standard of living. It's an ambitious vision, and one that few private philanthropies in Canada have taken on. McIsaac acknowledges it will be a long haul. But she believes Maytree is making headway. In Maytree's home community, the City of Toronto has committed to realizing the right to housing in its current ten-year plan to address the housing crisis and has agreed to establish a housing commissioner to hold the city accountable. "We are looking at how to build a human rights–based city and community," says McIsaac. "When human rights are built in as rules of the game, political winds can't blow the infrastructure away so easily. Building infrastructure and institutions is creating leverage for systemic change." Through its advocacy, networking, and active promotion of policy conversations, Maytree has shown how a focused philanthropic organization can have an influence in shaping the thinking of policy makers on poverty, immigration, diversity and inclusion, urban development, housing, and human rights.

Max Bell Foundation

In western Canada, there are fewer large and long-established private foundations than in the older financial centres of eastern Canada. Yet this smaller number of foundations is close-knit, and they share an attitude of pragmatic activism and community spirit. The province of Alberta is home to a group of innovative and influential private philanthropies. One of the group's leaders is Max Bell Foundation, created in 1972 by Max Bell, a man of many interests, as described by the foundation that bears his name, "a businessman, entrepreneur, oilman, newspaper publisher, sportsman, and philanthropist." As with so many of his philanthropic contemporaries in the 1950s and 1960s, he was a generous anonymous donor before he established his foundation. But the foundation was not to be led by him. Max Bell died prematurely at the age of fifty-nine shortly after the foundation was created and endowed with his gift of shares. The board of directors of the foundation, since its beginnings, has comprised people unrelated to Max Bell, except for his daughter and grandson. Max Bell left no specific direction to his foundation other than to give 30 per

cent of the amount awarded each year in grants to McGill University, half
of which goes to its Faculty of Medicine (Bell was a graduate of McGill).
Otherwise, his instructions to the founding board, made up of his trusted
friends and business associates, as well as a representative from McGill,
was to "do what you think should be done."

In its first twenty-five years, the foundation was based in Toronto
and gave to a range of charities across Canada. In 1997–98, as some of
the founding directors left the board, the foundation moved its base to
Calgary in the province where Max Bell had made his home and built
his fortune. The staff leadership was taken over by Dr David Elton, a
political scientist from University of Lethbridge who had been running
the Canada West Foundation, a policy think tank focused on western
Canada (and founded in 1970 with support from Max Bell). And the
foundation decided to put its attention specifically on innovations in
public policy. It came to this decision after a number of conversations
between the new president, Dr Elton, and the new chair, Ron Mannix,
another leading businessman from Calgary, who wanted to focus the
foundation's efforts, in the practical and innovative spirit of Max Bell,
where they could do the most good. According to Allan Northcott, the
current president of the foundation, who joined in 1998, it seemed to
Elton and Mannix that since governments are by far the largest funders
in the country, and have the most power to provide public goods, it was
logical to conclude that, to the extent [the foundation] wanted to have
impact, it should influence the policy agenda.[8] Having said this, it was
important to ask hard questions about what a private foundation could
do and to understand its role, strengths, and limitations in the wider
ecosystem of civil society. Dr Elton visited several foundation leaders in
the United States in the late 1990s to understand their strategies and to
help clarify the focus of Max Bell's work. One thing that became clear
was the important distinction between doing policy and doing politics (or
actively engaging in advocacy). The foundation decided that its interest
was not in putting policy ideas or initiatives on to the public agenda
through traditional policy advocacy but in helping bring the experience
and expertise of charities to bear on the issues already there. It decided
to focus on the process of public policy making, and the role of charities
in "giving good policy advice to governments."

The foundation quickly understood that many of the service delivery
agencies who typically had the expertise and the "on-the-ground" evidence

that could help shape public policy innovations were not set up to do policy work. Allan Northcott points out that this is an area in which charities are typically unskilled, noting that "many charities have unique hard data, research expertise, deep frontline experience, convening power, and 'campaign' skills, but relatively few have the skill and understanding required to effectively advocate to influence public policy."[9] This led the foundation to attempt a solution through small development grants in the range of $15,000 to $20,000 to help agencies in the community with scanning and project planning, which, in turn, could lead to a larger project grant from the foundation. In 2007, Max Bell decided to scale up its efforts and create a public policy training institute (PPTI) for community partners, modelled on the training program started by Maytree in Toronto in 2005. Max Bell began its PPTI with a regional focus on charities in Alberta, given the foundation's own limited staff capacity and the assumption that many policy issues are regional or local in nature.[10] The PPTI has now been operating as a program of the foundation for fifteen years as an annual six-month professional development program combining remote and in-person training in Calgary and Edmonton. Over 250 participants from 200 charities have been trained to develop, inform, and monitor public policy on issues of strategic importance to them. And Max Bell is allocating resources to develop and share more widely a public policy advocacy handbook for Canadian charities based on the curriculum of the PPTI. In addition to the PPTI, the foundation has created two other programs intended to foster the development of policy ideas and discussion: a Senior Fellows Program for experienced professionals to conduct research, write, and inform the public on policy questions; and a public speakers' series, PolicyForward, which gives practitioners and policymakers an opportunity to speak about emergent Canadian public policy issues. In 2018, Max Bell also aligned its annual contribution to McGill University with its overarching interest in public policy when it concluded a ten-year memorandum of understanding with the university to create the Max Bell Public Policy School. Most of the foundation's annual grants budget is now committed to charities engaging in public policy advocacy.

The foundation is disciplined in its approach to the types of policy issues it believes should be explored as priorities. Every three years it conducts an environmental scan that includes consulting with many senior public servants and policy experts. Since the late 1990s, it has highlighted

health, education, and the environment as key areas of interest. But priorities do shift within those broad sectors and the regular scanning helps the
foundation to align its program and granting priorities with government
priorities. For example, under "environment," the foundation is currently
interested in granting to develop strategies to help communities adapt to
the effects of climate change and to assist in the transition to a low-carbon
economy. Under "health," the foundation is interested in strategies to
improve the mental health of children and youth, and innovations in
health-care delivery. Under "education," it was interested in strategies
to prepare learners for digital citizenship and the knowledge economy
(since removed). And it applies two global thematic lenses to all its
granting priorities: improving the well-being of Indigenous individuals
and communities, and addressing the impacts of new technologies on
the structure and function of society and the economy, and on public
policy decision-making.

After twenty-odd years of granting and programming designed to
improve the quality of public policy making, the foundation can point
to concrete impact. Its grantees have succeeded in changing the quality
and impact of public policy in Alberta, particularly in the social services
field. But the foundation is reflecting on its experience and beginning
to experiment with a strategy designed for more collective action around
policy advocacy. As community partners have begun to work together more
frequently, in part through the experience many of their staff have had in
the PPTI, and as the complexity of the social and environmental problems
they are working on has increased, they and the foundation are seeing the
value and opportunity of collective action even across sectors. An example
of particular importance to Alberta today is planning for the transition
from an economy based on the combustion of hydrocarbons to one that
embraces the prospects of a net-zero future. Collaborative thinking on
policies to foster this transition is emerging among universities, think
tanks, government policy units, and environmental non-profits. Max Bell
is playing a role in catalyzing the process of collaborative development of
policy options in this field. Another example that Max Bell has supported
financially is the Calgary Social Policy Collaborative, a loose network of
forty or more community organizations, many of which are led by staff
who have been through the PPTI. This group is working on collective
policy thinking around income security and poverty reduction. Max Bell
Foundation has also consistently supported policy advocacy efforts for the

charitable sector through its grants to multi-member umbrella organizations such as Imagine Canada and Philanthropic Foundations Canada.

While public policy advocacy work is difficult to measure and
evaluate, given the long lead times and multiple decision-makers, Max
Bell Foundation can be justified in thinking it has had an impact on
policy development in Alberta and on behalf of the charitable sector
nationally, judging by the increase in capacity, networking, and policy
infrastructure in the sector. In focusing on innovation, skills building,
and policy advocacy through multiple channels, Max Bell is occupying an
important niche. "Every foundation should figure out what it is best at,"
concludes Allan Northcott. "What we are doing is a good reflection of
what Max Bell can be best at because this is what we know, this is the
expertise we have."[11]

The Muttart Foundation

Bob Wyatt didn't plan on a career in philanthropy. In the 1980s he was
working as a professional journalist and public relations expert. In 1986,
the board of the Muttart Foundation of Edmonton invited Wyatt to
speak to them about their mission and how to communicate it more
effectively. Wyatt informed them in his characteristically direct style that
they and their mission were unknown. "You need to figure out your
message and who you want to communicate with," he told them. The
board turned around and invited him to become a director to help them
do just that. Two years later, in 1989, they offered him the job of executive
director, asking him to develop a new strategy for the foundation. He
took it on, pursuing a mission that would become more proactive, higher
profile, closer to the charities that Muttart wanted as partners, and more
deliberate in selecting projects. This was a transformation for the foundation, which, since its founding in 1953 by successful entrepreneur and
businessman Merrill Muttart and his wife, Gladys, had been a quiet but
generous donor, funding a typical range of institutions, such as universities
and hospitals (many outside of Alberta), and causes, such as diabetes
prevention, cardiac research, and social services, as well as literacy and
clean water projects outside of Canada. The foundation was private but
not dominated by family interests. Gladys and Merrill Muttart died within
three months of each other, in 1969 and 1970, and their wills endowed
the foundation, while their son continued as a director on the board.

But the Muttarts left no restrictions or instructions, leaving the foundation simply "to improve the human condition."

Wyatt began to develop a clearer scope for the foundation's work. From his first days as executive director, he believed in the foundation's philosophy that it should be "a venture capital supplier for the sector ... prepared to take risks to fund unknown things and take the possibility of failure."[12] Within this philosophical framework, he established programmatic and geographic guidelines, narrowing the scope of Muttart's granting to Alberta, Saskatchewan, and the Yukon and Northwest Territories. However, there was an important exception. Wyatt's view, which has been encapsulated in the mission of the Muttart Foundation, is that a robust charitable sector is central to a strong, healthy society. To build such a robust sector you need to invest in networks, leaders, and the regulatory frameworks and public policies that shape the sector's work throughout Canada. Muttart began in the mid-1990s to fund work by the Canadian Centre for Philanthropy (now Imagine Canada), which had a policy arm headed by Gordon Floyd. In 1997, Wyatt and Floyd put together an unprecedented initiative with Carl Juneau, a senior federal official in the Charities Directorate of the CRA. They agreed to convene a group of Canadian and international experts to meet over two days in private with federal policy makers from the CRA to work out a policy on community economic development as a charitable purpose. Three or four months after the meeting, CRA issued a first draft policy on this topic. Wyatt realized that he had something. This was a way for Muttart to start having an impact at a national level on a federal public policy framework, the *Income Tax Act* and regulations, of enormous importance to the charitable sector. His realization, and the support of his board, led Wyatt to initiate a unique series of semi-annual private convenings between sector leaders and experts and federal Finance Canada and CRA officials to discuss aspects of the tax regime. By 2022, these so-called "Muttart consultations" will have taken place over fifty times. They have built important relationships of trust between the government and sector leaders. In the view of one of its regular participants, "There is no change in charity regulatory policy that has been enacted in the last decade that didn't start [at the consultation]."[13] Part of the reason for their success is that Muttart itself has never had a specific agenda. It has asked participants to come to the table without agendas themselves, and under strict obligation to keep the conversations inside the room. Public summaries of the consultations are anonymized. This is an effort to create space and opportunity to listen, learn, and debate different points of view on charity regulatory issues. "We use our convening power and reputation to bring together people with disparate views from everywhere in the world," notes Wyatt. "Our goal is to have them come together in fruitful exchanges around common problems."

Muttart has used many other strategies to strengthen policy capacity in the charitable sector in Canada, and to foster knowledge and understanding of policy issues affecting the sector, particularly regulatory issues. The foundation has been a long-standing core supporter of Imagine Canada's efforts to coordinate, inform, and speak on behalf of the sector nationally. Muttart has also been active in its home province of Alberta, encouraging and supporting discussions that led to the creation of regional umbrellas, such as the Edmonton and Calgary Chambers of Voluntary Organizations. While Muttart does not have an agenda in its convenings around specific policy issues in charity regulation, it has not hesitated to create opportunities to advance charity law through other means, such as funding a separate organization, the Pemsel Case Foundation, to investigate, research, and promote judicial and legal developments in charity law in Canada. Wyatt himself has been personally engaged as a co-chair of the Joint Regulatory Table, a sector-government effort in the early 2000s to review and improve CRA interactions with charities; as a regular faculty member for the Max Bell PPTI; and as a co-editor of a book on charity regulatory policy across five common law jurisdictions, now in wide circulation among policy makers and researchers. Over a thirty-three-year career of philanthropic leadership, Wyatt and his successive boards have built the Muttart Foundation as a unique and significant contributor to the development of federal policy on charities with the goal of "making things better" for all registered charities. This impact extends to Muttart's second policy field of interest: early childhood learning and development. In this area, too, the foundation has focused on supporting early childhood and care charities to "play a full role in the development of public policy related to early childhood education and care." As in the field of charity regulation, Muttart sees its role as funding the capacity of umbrella organizations in the child-care field. It also supports work on policy approaches to the funding and development of early childhood education and care, and on how best to build leadership and management capacity in early childhood organizations, especially in Alberta. Through persistence, and single-minded conviction, Wyatt has transformed the Muttart Foundation since the 1990s. There would be no doubt in the minds of policy makers, community partners, and philanthropic peers today about Muttart's mission and approach.

Conclusion

What do these three examples tell us about private philanthropy and public policy? Certainly, that private philanthropy can be deployed with great impact to help change public policy across many fields. None of the three foundations, Maytree, Max Bell, and Muttart, have large endowments or very large staff. But they share certain traits that might explain their impact: thoughtful and determined leadership, clarity on role, proactivity in setting priorities and choosing partners, courage to innovate by creating or funding others to create new content and platforms, and a willingness to be visible in a way that opens them potentially to criticism. All three could be challenged on their legitimacy to engage in the public policy arena, given their status as private philanthropies. All three have countered this by being open about their objectives and approaches; their leaders have all spoken in public about why, what, and how they are working to make public policy better. Maytree has gone further than the other two in making clear its policy stance and belief in the direction of change through its focus on human rights. Max Bell and Muttart have been less assertive in stating a policy option preference but have worked to strengthen the voices of those who clearly do have a point of view on change.

In his 2015 book *Public Good by Private Means: How Philanthropy shapes Britain*, UK observer Rhodri Davies suggests that all philanthropy engages in policy advocacy, even if this is not explicitly acknowledged:

A key distinguishing feature of philanthropy is that it has a purpose or goal. In most cases this can be framed as a problem that needs to be overcome or a change that needs to be made in society. By giving to a particular cause, a philanthropist is expressing a view about a way in which our society, our laws or government policies need to be different. This is an inherently political act. It is only if we incorrectly conflate "political" and "party political" that there is

a problem. If we instead reclaim the proper understanding of what
the sphere of politics includes, then it is clear that philanthropy
is and always has been a valuable tool for people to express their
beliefs within that sphere.[14]

In this sense, Maytree, Max Bell, and Muttart are simply more explicit
and more focused in their choice of strategies and target audiences. Other
private foundations are starting to raise their voices, express a view on a
needed policy change, or engage with others in attempts to influence policy
directly, in some cases through direct collaborations with governments.
The urgency of the issues affecting communities, the country, and our
world suggest that private philanthropy has no choice but to step forward,
with all the obligations of transparency and accountability this entails.
In the next chapter, I describe the work of three private foundations that
have taken on one of the most urgent policy challenges of all: how to
deal with the climate emergency.

Confronting Climate Change

The Ivey Foundation, the Donner Canadian Foundation, the Trottier Family Foundation

The climate crisis upends all predictability. Climate change equals human change, and it requires reimagining our lives. So how should we all live with the growing risk of disaster?

Simon Kuper, *Financial Times* (3 and 4 July 2021)

At the end of 2019, Mark Carney, former governor of the Bank of Canada and the Bank of England, and UN special envoy on Climate Change and Climate Finance, spoke to the global commitment to achieve a net-zero carbon economy by 2050. He challenged the financial industry: "A question for every company, every financial institution, every asset manager, pension fund or insurer: What's your plan?"[1] This question is also one for every foundation or philanthropic organization in the face of the climate emergency: What's your plan for contributing to net-zero (carbon) by 2050? It's a question the Ivey Foundation, a third-generation family foundation, has asked itself with urgency. How does a relatively small foundation begin to move the needle on this enormously difficult problem?

The Ivey Foundation was created by Richard G. Ivey and his son Richard M. Ivey in the late 1940s. Four members of the third generation of the Ivey family sit on the board of what is still very much a family foundation more than seventy years after its founding. By 2005, the foundation had been granting for several decades to environmental causes, most notably conservation and biodiversity. The family was increasingly interested in boreal forest conservation, given Canada's enormous forest resources, and conservation's importance to the environment, biodiversity, and carbon storage for the planet. When the position of president came vacant in 2002, with the departure of the first non-family staff leader, Marvi Ricker, who had led the foundation since 1990, the Iveys turned to someone with a track record in the environmental movement. This was Bruce Lourie, co-founder and president of Summerhill Group, a firm specializing in energy sustainability and non-profit management. Through Summerhill Group, Lourie had been instrumental in the creation of several non-profit organizations, including the Canadian Environmental Grantmakers' Network (now Environment Funders Canada), the Canadian Energy Efficiency Alliance (now Efficiency Canada), and the Sustainability Network, a capacity-building organization for environmental non-governmental organizations. Another Canadian foundation, the Laidlaw Foundation of Toronto, had given Lourie his start in environmental philanthropy by contracting him to run their first environmental granting program and by supporting his efforts to create the Sustainability Network, efforts inspired by an American private foundation, the Mott Foundation, to build the skills of local environmental organizations around the Great Lakes. Lourie's work with the Laidlaw Foundation, together with his sustainable energy consulting expertise, spawned the campaign to phase out coal-fired power plants in Ontario, North America's largest climate change action.

When Lourie arrived at the Ivey Foundation, in 2005, he began to connect with other funders and environmental non-profits around an ambitious strategy to negotiate directly with the forest industry on forest and wildlife conservation. This work led to the signing in 2010 of a significant pact, the Canadian Boreal Forest Agreement, between the Forest Products Association of Canada and nine environmental groups, including the Ivey Foundation. But the climate challenge was becoming ever more pressing as the second decade of the twenty-first century began. It was time for the foundation to refocus. What more could a small private foundation do to help "green the economy"? Its answer was to look at *both* the economy and the environment, with climate change at the nexus.

The most challenging systemic crisis the world faces today is climate change and its consequences. It is a border-crossing and complex threat, with many impacts on our health, economic prospects, social systems, and individual well-being. Any foundation with a concern for the well-being of communities should be concerned about climate change, even if the foundation's goals do not include a focus on the environment, science, or climate. If there is any area where the consequences of inaction today will create enormous injustice for generations in the not-too-distant future, it is this. If there is any place where a foundation can apply the advantages of its high-risk tolerance, ability to support innovation, and capacity to provide long-term funding, it is here. We face enormous disruptions caused by climate change to communities, jobs, our urban and rural environment, and our quality of life in this decade of the 2020s. Parts of Canada are warming at twice the global rate. Global economies must evolve quickly to a low- or zero-carbon emissions world. This is a big, painful, and complex transition. Transition is the word that will resonate most in the years of this decade. And it is the word philanthropy must grapple with, in all its messiness.

How can we navigate the transition, and help communities mitigate and/or adapt to the impacts of climate change? Disruption can be mitigated. Communities can be helped to adapt. Yet few Canadian foundations have taken up climate change work explicitly yet as part of their funding. On the other hand, a larger and growing number are considering climate change impacts as they make their investment decisions, and more of them are using environmental impact criteria in deciding what to include in their investment portfolios. Among those that are using their granting directly to focus on climate mitigation and adaptation, there are several possible strategies: funding climate-related projects and programs; building and supporting policy development and advocacy platforms; supporting collaborative mechanisms for pooling funds; working jointly with public and private sector partners; and funding grassroots action for climate justice and resilience within communities. In this chapter I describe three private foundations that are working with a mix of these strategic approaches to climate change mitigation and adaptation. The Ivey Foundation has chosen to create new institutions and networks designed to fill gaps in Canada's policy capability to transition its economy to net zero. The Trottier Family Foundation has followed the lead of Ivey, working at the local level on the transition to low- or zero-carbon emissions, and, at a national level, like Ivey, to build new networks and entities. The Donner Canadian Foundation is deploying its assets through collaboration to accelerate efforts to protect marine environments and steward land, as well as to mitigate and adapt to climate change. All three of these foundations are working with other funders. The climate crisis is far too large and complex a crisis for foundations to work alone. Several Canadian private funder collaborative initiatives were launched over the last decade, including the Clean Economy Fund and the Low Carbon Funders Group. Much has been learned and work has been accelerated through these collaborations. But there is no doubt the urgency of the work is growing in parallel with the urgency of the climate emergency.

The Ivey Foundation

In 2014, after three years of reflection on its previous work in forest conservation and environmental sustainability, Ivey launched a bold initiative on both the economy and the environment. Its new vision statement made this link explicit: "To help create a shared vision for Canada's future – one that integrates economy and environment, achieves resource efficiency, and fosters innovation and investment for a smarter, sustainable economy."[2] Unusually for a private foundation, Ivey crafted and made public a strategic framework for a program it intends to pursue for ten years. Ivey's framework is explicit about desired outcomes and the granting strategies that will be used to achieve them. According to the foundation, "This Framework is a tool to help focus grant decision-making while also allowing the Program to evolve over time. It is also meant to assist external stakeholders and potential grantees in better understanding the Program and the ways in which it may align with their own organization's activities."[3] Three outcomes are identified as "systemic change drivers": appropriate *pricing* of environmental costs, innovative *investing* to develop resource-efficient business and infrastructure, and accurate *measuring* of well-being beyond traditional GDP measures. Ivey made clear it intended to work to bring about change in all these drivers.

Climate change is at the heart of Ivey's thinking about a sustainable future. The complexities of the systems that will need to be mobilized to confront climate change require effort on many fronts. "We (Ivey) are in the 'systems change' business," as Lourie puts it. "Any systems change has to be approached through multiple strategies ... it's important not to limit one's understanding of foundation strategies as being just about social justice, or just about advocacy or just about supporting institutions, or just about funding what is innovative. It may be necessary to pursue all these strategies to tackle the major challenge of climate change."[4] Since 2014, Ivey has allocated a significant portion of its annual granting budget to the creation of eight institutions and collaborations that, in its words, are designed to "fill what we saw as gaps in Canada's capacity to research, understand, communicate, and overcome fundamental barriers to transitioning the economy."[5] These initiatives range from policy research think tanks to inter-university research and teaching collaboratives, to energy data and analysis portals, to funder collaboratives. In every instance, the foundation was entering into and filling gaps in policy infrastructure. Says Lourie, "When we started doing this, we saw that no one was thinking about this integrated approach [to environment and economy]. There were few think tanks or academic-based centres with this focus. There was a lack of institutional capacity to do policy thinking about how to make the transition. We did not know where we could find the partners to work with. We had to find them or create them or collaborate with others. The task was to figure out how to give the dollars away, not simply to give them away."

As Ivey implements its Economy and Environment Program, it has directed about 80 per cent of its funding to university-based partners with the goal, Lourie says, of "trying to take academics out of their trad-itional research roles and bring them into policy work." In each case, the grant was used to create something that hadn't existed before. Canada's Ecofiscal Commission, based at McGill University, developed new policy ideas around carbon pricing. The Transition Accelerator, launched at Carleton University as a collaboration among researchers, government, and industry, is developing transition pathways for major energy and socio-technical systems. The Institute for Sustainable Finance, a national business school collaboration based at Queen's University, is developing options for financing the transition to a sustainable economy. Lourie notes that, "The Foundation does not see itself now solely as a grantmaker. [We spend] 20 per cent of time on grants and 80 per cent of time on support to institutions, using three content experts [on staff]." The foundation has seven staff, of which three are full time.

Ivey has not neglected the investing side of its activities, pursuing a ten-year strategy under the leadership of the foundation's chair, Rosamond Ivey, to "incrementally shift the portfolio's allocation to investments that prioritize sustainability as a core value."[6] At the end of 2019, Ivey's sustain-able investing exposure was at 28 per cent of its portfolio, an amount significantly larger than that of most other Canadian private foundations. The foundation's thinking about the evolution and assessment of its strategies in funding and investing has been described in detail in the foundation's public annual reports.[7] Ivey was one of the first Canadian foundations to issue an annual report over fifty years ago. In these reports, particularly since 2014, Ivey has detailed not only its grants and financial data but also the evolution of its strategic reflection and learning over time. The reports provide insight on the foundation's highly structured approach in a way that is considerably more transparent than one finds in most private foundations.

Knowing that it needed to stretch its philanthropic resources and leverage more activity and impact, Ivey reached out to others as it had before in pushing for the Boreal Forest Agreement. In 2014, Ivey invited a few Canadian foundations to the table to discuss the creation of a new Clean Economy Fund (CEF). CEF is a collective funder group with approximately a dozen foundations and funds as partners. It was structured as a separate charitable entity to act as a "re-granter" of philanthropic funds dedicated to working on approaches to transition to a clean and sustainable economy. Ivey's initiative to bring together funders for collective action mirrors the ever more urgent efforts being made in the United States and globally to deploy philanthropy against climate change. Since the Paris Agreement of 2015, more collective funding pools have been set up, as well as initiatives to guide new funders into climate change work, and commitments by funder networks to self-educate, coordinate funding opportunities, and measure and report progress. An International Philanthropy Commitment on Climate Change was launched in 2021 to enlist foundations around the world in committing more funds. Inspired by this, in October 2021 the four major funder networks in Canada invited funders to sign a Canadian Philanthropy Commitment on Climate Change and commit to specific targets and actions to meet those targets. The Canadian Philanthropy Commitment had forty funder signatories as of early 2022.

The Donner Canadian Foundation

The Donner Canadian Foundation, like the Ivey Foundation, is one of Canada's oldest private foundations. Originally established in 1950 in Montreal by American philanthropist William Donner, who had moved to Canada, the foundation continues to be led by Donner's descendants, who live in the United States. The foundation governance structure involves a large membership of about thirty Donner relatives from five separate families. This group includes third, fourth, and even fifth generation members of the family who engage through annual meetings, rotations on the board of directors, and participation in sub-groups, which meet regularly on topics of shared philanthropic interest. The youngest

generation (in their late twenties or early thirties) are being introduced to
the philanthropic work of the foundation through organized education
and mentoring activities. Although its asset size ranks it in the top fifty
of large private grantmaking foundations in Canada, Donner has chosen
to maintain a very lean operation. It functions with a small full-time staff
of three based in Toronto. The foundation has remained firmly rooted in
Canada and the family members, even if based in the United States, have
taken a continuing interest in Canadian issues. Through a long-standing
commitment to Canadian public policy research, Donner has become one
of the most important funders of Canadian policy think tanks. As well,
Donner manages two programs to recognize and foster excellence in public
policy thinking and debate, including an annual book prize to celebrate
outstanding public policy writing by Canadians, and a semi-annual public
lecture series featuring some of the world's most prominent intellectuals.

Public policy research and debate is not Donner's principal funding
focus today, however. The foundation devotes the largest portion of its
granting budget to environmental conservation, including, more recently,
the transition to clean energy and a sustainable economy. Donner's
interest in environmental conservation dates to the early 2000s when
the family members began to engage with the US Nature Conservancy
and made some grants in Canada for the purchase and conservation
of environmentally sensitive land. This interest became more focused
over the next decade on marine conservation, with the foundation
supporting marine and fisheries protection efforts particularly in the
Atlantic regions of Canada through grants to Oceana Canada, Oceans
North, the Ecology Action Centre, and the World Wildlife Fund, among
many other grantees. Environmental conservation for the foundation
has encompassed land, water, wildlife, and ecosystems. Environmental
granting has been consistently the largest part of its portfolio in the last
few years. In 2020, for example, it devoted 35 per cent of its granting to
environment and wildlife stewardship and protection.[8] Donner has also
been a long-standing member of Environment Funders Canada (EFC).
Through the EFC, Donner participates in the Oceans Collaborative, which
pools funds for small grants to conservation and stewardship of marine
and coastal ecosystems.

Given the interests of the family in environmental issues, it was inevitable the foundation would begin to take a more active funding role in
addressing the challenges posed by climate change. Some members of the

family were particularly interested in carbon pricing and incentives to move toward low- or zero-carbon emissions. But the foundation had no expertise or track record in engaging with organizations working toward a low-carbon economy. Just as this issue was being raised by some family members in 2016, the Ivey Foundation invited Donner staff and board members to a gathering of Canadian foundations in Montebello, Quebec, to launch the CEF. Donner's executive director, Helen McLean, recalls that meeting as a key event in the decision to join the CEF at the earliest stage. One of the family members, Bob Spencer, attended the retreat with her and championed the collective fund to his fellow directors as "a fit with the strategic goal set by the family members."[9] Spencer was so enthusiastic about the CEF that he subsequently joined its board of directors. Since 2016, Donner has been one of the largest contributors to the CEF, granting over $1.7 million over five years. These funds flow through the CEF to align funder support around new convening and communication structures, such as Efficiency Canada and the Transition Accelerator.

At this stage, Donner, unlike Ivey, is not looking to change its approach as a grantmaker. It functions primarily as a manager of arms-length grants to diverse organizations, both large and small, numbering on average about seventy-give per year. But the foundation clearly identifies collaborative funding as a way to stretch its resources and impact, particularly in the area of climate change. McLean suggests that the foundation's experience with the CEF is emblematic of its current thinking about its work. "The evolution of the foundation's strategy towards collective and collaborative environments has been slow but deliberate ... our confidence has grown and the context has changed," she notes. "Now, launching work completely separately from others in the foundation community would seem jarring."

The Trottier Family Foundation

A third family foundation has taken a more activist lead in the climate change fight. In its 2019 budget, the federal government announced a $183 million investment in Low Carbon Cities Canada (LC3), a partnership between seven urban centres and the Federation of Canadian Municipalities (FCM) intended to enable and accelerate urban carbon-reduction solutions. In August 2019, the government allocated $32.5 million of this investment for the establishment of the Greater Montreal Climate Fund to support the development of low-carbon solutions in the Montreal

metropolitan region. The Trottier Family Foundation took on its implementation. Why would a private family foundation incubate itself a new
organization to work on urban carbon reduction at a city level? This is an
approach that goes well beyond grantmaking or funding others to do the
work on climate change mitigation. The story of how Trottier became so
directly involved in launching a new player on urban carbon reduction
illustrates the way in which private foundations can step in to play a
catalytic role in building solutions to climate change.

It begins in 2000 when the Trottier Family Foundation was established
in Montreal by Lorne Trottier and Louise Rousselle Trottier. From the
start, the foundation took an interest in scientific inquiry. Lorne Trottier is
an engineer, business entrepreneur, and innovator with a lifelong interest
in the impact of science and technology on society. Through his foundation, he made significant gifts to McGill University in Montreal, from
which he graduated. These grants were intended to help build McGill's
capacity in electrical and aerospace engineering and astrophysics, and
to foster science education and the promotion of the understanding of
science by the public. While not specifically addressed to climate change,
the record of the foundation before 2016 suggests that sustainability
was becoming a key area of concern. In 2012, two major gifts totalling
$15 million to McGill went toward creating an Institute for Sustainability
in Engineering and Design and for endowing an Institute for Science
and Public Policy. This reflected Lorne Trottier's belief in the critical
importance of supporting researchers and shaping public understanding
of science and technology, with a broader goal of influencing public policy
on sustainability. Trottier also credits his two daughters, Sylvie and Claire,
both trained as scientists, for shaping his thinking about the growing
importance of addressing climate change. The work of the foundation
on climate change since 2015 has now positioned it to be one of the most
active and engaged Canadian private funders on climate.

After fifteen years with no staff, the foundation took a significant
step by engaging a full-time executive director, Eric St-Pierre, in 2016.
The Trottiers and their daughters, who sat on the foundation board, also
articulated a public mission for the foundation that specifically identified
mitigating climate change as one of its areas of concern: "Our mission is
to support organizations that work towards the advancement of scientific
inquiry, the promotion of education, fostering better health, protecting
the environment and mitigating climate change."[10] In addition, reflecting

the entrepreneurial and innovation mindset of its founders, the mission statement identified Trottier's approach as being a risk-taker and catalyzer of innovation and collaboration. Two private foundation leaders helped to shape the thinking of the Trottier Foundation as it began to accelerate its efforts. Stephen Huddart of the McConnell Foundation and Bruce Lourie of Ivey were brought in by St-Pierre to speak to the foundation board and share their perspectives on the roles of a private foundation. Lourie spoke to the board and St-Pierre about the work of the Ivey Foundation to build pathways to a more sustainable economy. As he shared the example of Ivey, the Trottiers' interest was piqued. They asked themselves how their foundation could help to catalyze efforts to fund and scale up low-carbon solutions in cities and in the wider areas of transportation, industrial emissions, finance, and energy production. From the beginning, St-Pierre and the Trottiers saw this work as collaborative. St-Pierre joined the table at the CEF. Sylvie Trottier comments that "philanthropy is not a competitive game. ... Foundations can work on issues and projects together, particularly on complex issues like climate change which can't be addressed by foundations working alone. It's one thing to fund large institutions such as hospitals or universities with one-to-one funder to grantee grants. But climate change requires intersectoral and inter-foundation collaboration."[11] By 2015, Lorne Trottier had begun a collaboration with the David Suzuki Foundation around urban climate change solutions. In 2018, the foundation participated in a public-private partnership agreement with the City of Montreal to develop a plan to make the city carbon-neutral. This agreement was co-signed by the Trottier Foundation, the David Suzuki Foundation, the City of Montreal, and the C40 Cities Climate Leadership Group.[12] The role of the Trottier Foundation is to finance the technical modelling by scientists that could amplify the city's limited capacities to create more detailed plans of action for reducing emissions.

At around the same time, St-Pierre was actively working on a plan to replicate in Montreal the model of the Atmospheric Fund (TAF), a regional climate agency created and endowed by the City of Toronto in 1991 to finance local initiatives to combat climate change and improve air quality in the Greater Toronto Area. In 2017, Trottier commissioned an independent study to determine the need for a similar agency in Montreal. Confirming that the need was there, and that successful replication required a template or business model, Trottier worked with TAF to organize regional consultations in Toronto and Vancouver with environmental organizations, community organizations, city representatives, academics, and others to develop interest in the TAF model. In doing so, Trottier was deploying its convening resources, a tool that is uniquely suited to the independent private foundation. The collaboration of TAF and Trottier led directly to the creation of LC3 in May 2017 as a network that supports a replication or adaptation of the TAF model in seven different cities – Halifax, Montreal, Ottawa, Toronto, Edmonton, Calgary, and Vancouver – in partnership with the FCM. After intense advocacy efforts by the partners, including Trottier, the federal government awarded $183 million to LC3, combined with a $1 billion endowment to the FCM for the Green Municipal Fund.

The Trottier Family Foundation is now involved in the incubation of the LC3 centre for Montreal, the Greater Montreal Climate Fund (GMCF). This direct engagement is part of how the foundation sees its role as catalyst and facilitator. According to the LC3 network itself, much credit is due to Trottier's efforts. "From grants towards the consultation process, legal and communication expenses, to government relations, in-kind support, and start-up costs for the GMCF, St-Pierre and his team have spent countless hours and many dollars since 2016 to make this initiative a reality."[13] St-Pierre also believes that working with other LC3 centres will benefit the foundation as it thinks about next steps. An LC3 profile of his work as a climate leader quotes his views on reciprocal learning: "I'm hoping to learn what other Centres are doing and bring some of our work [in Montreal] to the table. … For example, it would be great to establish a program in Montreal that is focused on building retrofits and energy-efficiency projects, and then share that with other LC3 Centres, so they can implement their own programs in their communities."[14]

In parallel with the work to launch the GMCF, St-Pierre and the foundation took an important next step to expand on the C40 collaboration with the City of Montreal begun in 2018. In late 2020, Trottier and the Foundation of Greater Montreal (FGM) came together to announce the Montreal Climate Partnership (MCP), a multi-sectoral initiative bringing together organizations from the public, private, philanthropic, and community sectors with the aim of mobilizing the city's key players in support of its goals to reduce greenhouse gas emissions by 55 per cent by 2030 and achieve carbon neutrality by 2050. Trottier committed $600,000 to this $1.6 million mobilization effort, built on international models to foster dialogue and push for efforts led by civil society to reduce greenhouse gas emissions in the city. This kind of mobilization effort is still highly unusual for a private foundation in Canada, but, arguably, the difficulty and urgency of the climate change challenge requires it. In launching the initiative, St-Pierre said that international examples such as the City of Boston inspired their work. The media release quoted him: "Across the globe, philanthropic foundations play a vital part in supporting cities to adopt ambitious climate plans ... Montréal is no exception. ... The challenge now is to mobilize all of Montréal's leaders to achieve our climate objectives. Our hope is that the MCP will be able to help speed up the city's decarbonization through teamwork and concerted action."[15]

The Trottier Family Foundation is a member of the Low Carbon Funders Group, a collaborative of Canadian foundations and national environmental organizations supported by EFC. This group is sharing learning and trying to align funding around initiatives in line with the Pan-Canadian Framework on Clean Growth and Climate Change developed by the federal government with the provinces and territories and in consultation with Indigenous Peoples. This framework involves pricing carbon pollution, reducing carbon emissions, strengthening community resilience and adaptation to climate change, and investing in clean technology innovations. St-Pierre is clear that one of the most effective approaches to the foundation's work is to collaborate with others, including funders, community organizations, and all levels of government, to find solutions, people, and ideas. He is wary of "philanthropic imperialism," or what occurs when a foundation decides that it knows more and better.[16] That said, he acknowledges this work requires a commitment of time that is onerous for foundations with smaller staff, such as Trottier. Throughout the process of building the LC3 network, St-Pierre worked with only two other full-time staff and had to be prepared to respond quickly and to be flexible in meeting the shifting goals and managing the conversations needed to succeed in a multi-partner effort. He acknowledges it could be messy and time-consuming. Nevertheless, he is emphatic on the advantages of collaboration: meeting peers and other collaborators, getting to know decision-makers, gaining expertise, co-funding or leveraging additional funds, and working in a funder ecosystem.

Trottier is deploying a wide range of strategies in addressing climate change mitigation. Most of them have not been tried before. This is consistent with the foundation's view that it is able and, indeed, compelled to take risks and innovate. As St-Pierre puts it, "It is ironic that philanthropy is risk averse because foundations are often started by entrepreneurs who took a lot of risks in business – why should they be conservative in philanthropy?" In his view, foundations have an accountability to provide public benefit. The best way they can do that is to bring their resources to the testing of new ideas and approaches. "We should not be afraid to fail." Trottier, much like Ivey, is looking at the broader systems that determine our ability to step up as a country to the climate change emergency, and it is trying to pull on many levers at once. As Sylvie Trottier puts it, "We need to fund multiple pieces of the puzzle. And look at what pieces are not being funded. We fund both grassroots projects and policy development, as well as funding big institutions like universities."[17] The impact of the pandemic has also focused the foundation's attention on the linkages between its work on climate change and its interest in promoting health, with greater focus on the underlying socio-economic inequalities that create such injustice in the distribution of negative impacts from climate and health crises.

Foundations and Climate Change: What Next?

Less than 2 per cent of global philanthropy goes to mitigating climate change.[18] But the challenge looms larger than ever. The Canadian government has committed to achieving net-zero carbon emissions by 2050, with some aggressive targets to be met even earlier. Is that sufficient? Is Canadian philanthropy playing its part? Not yet, not enough, according to Ivey and Trottier. More funders need to have an answer to Mark Carney's urgent question: What are *you* doing to get to net zero? There are plenty of opportunities. Collective efforts such as the Low Carbon Funders Group, LC3, and the Canadian Philanthropy Commitment on Climate Change are picking up momentum. The Trottier Family Foundation funded a report for EFC in September 2020 that summarized gaps and opportunities for Canada's philanthropic sector in funding Canada's low-carbon future. This report provided a clear framework for identifying opportunities for philanthropic action and a menu of strategies to engage. It concludes that cross-cutting efforts are going to be critical if philanthropy is going to have any impact in mobilizing the action that is required over the next ten years on climate change. These efforts "range from developing and adhering to a climate accountability framework, co-creating a just transition, fostering public mobilization, pricing carbon, and shifting investments."[19] And much of this work must be done in collaboration with or under the guidance of Indigenous Peoples, the original protectors of the land, waters, and animals found in Canada. The Metcalf Foundation of Toronto, for example, is pursuing a strategy focused on helping Canada achieve its commitment to protect and conserve 30 per cent of lands and waters by 2030. Metcalf is focusing its so-called 30×30 effort through support for Indigenous leadership on the ground to protect peatlands in the Hudson Bay Lowlands and the Mackenzie River Basin. Metcalf is also doing what a foundation can do best to add value to the effort: research and inform the design of new strategies, convene cross-sectoral players, and build public awareness and support for the importance of conserving peatlands, grasslands, and old-growth forests. The work of Ivey, Trottier, Donner, Metcalf and many others will have to expand greatly if philanthropy is going to play up to its potential to catalyze more capital, more ideas, and more activity into the increasingly urgent transition. Every funder in Canada should have an answer to Carney's question: What are *we* doing to get to net zero? Eric St-Pierre sums it up crisply: "If we don't figure out climate, nothing else matters. It compromises work across all sectors."

8

Partnering for Impact

*The Graham Boeckh Foundation, the Helderleigh
Foundation, the Azrieli Foundation*

Together, we nurture networks, helping people and communities discover
their strengths and maximize their potential by connecting them to
resources, expertise and education.

Dr Naomi Azrieli

In 1986, the Boeckh family of Montreal suffered a tragedy. Graham
Boeckh, the twenty-two-year-old eldest son, died from medical compli-
cations related to schizophrenia. He and his family had struggled for
years with efforts to find diagnosis and treatment options for his illness.
When Graham turned eighteen, overnight he found himself considered
an adult by the health system, no longer able to access the care offered
by pediatrists geared to serve youth under the age of eighteen. His family
was able to help him find new care options, although, as an adult, his
health-care providers could not involve his family. But many young adults
with a mental illness can't negotiate their way through a baffling and
fragmented system. Graham's father, Tony, an economist and a business
entrepreneur, was used to finding solutions; he had started and built
organizations to meet information needs and gaps in financial markets.
In the years after Graham's death, Tony and his family turned their
entrepreneurial energies and resources to philanthropy with a single and
ambitious purpose: to change the Canadian mental health-care system,
to help save lives, and to improve outcomes for Canadian families whose
members, particularly youth, suffered a mental illness. The Graham
Boeckh Foundation was created as a private foundation in 1990. Thirty
years later, the Boeckhs remain deeply engaged in pursuing their purpose.
Tony Boeckh serves as chair of the board of the foundation and his son
Ian is its full-time president.

The goal of the Boeckh Foundation is to catalyze transformative changes that significantly improve the lives of young people at risk of or living with mental illness. Over three decades since its creation, the foundation has evolved in significant ways. It is focused on Canada but is also promoting global philanthropic collaboration on youth mental health. It supports individual research projects and also the pooling and exchange of knowledge generated through research. It makes grants and it also convenes, documents, and advocates. From its early days in the 1990s, when it focused on funding academic chairs in schizophrenia research, to its current strategies focused on moving research results more quickly to the young people who could benefit, the Boeckh Foundation has been willing to take on new roles. Its purpose is clear: to bring about a faster development of integrated youth mental health services. From the beginning, according to Ian Boeckh, the foundation's view has been that the end goal is the most important thing. Their starting and ending point is meeting the needs of young people. "We work back from the question of 'what do *we* want' to 'what do we need to do to get to what *they* want,'" says Ian. "This distinguishes us from other foundations."[1] Ian Boeckh is firm that the work they do is not about them but about what they can do to help society address the complex issues around youth access to mental health treatment.

The Boeckh Foundation knows it can't do its work in isolation. In the first decade of the foundation's work, Tony Boeckh spoke to many people working in the field of mental health, asking them questions about possible approaches to research and to patient care. In 2006, after fifteen years of funding schizophrenia researchers, Tony and Ian Boeckh decided to be more proactive. In 2012, after exploration and discussion, they took a risk and set up an unprecedented philanthropic partnership with the Canadian Institutes of Health Research (CIHR), the federal funding agency for medical research. The Boeckh Foundation was taking the first step on a path it would walk consistently in partnership with others, not alone.

It's now commonplace to hear people quote the proverbial statement: "You go fast alone but you go far with others." If we understand "going far" as getting to a solution to a complicated problem or having more impact on more people, then "going with others" is an essential strategy for foundations. "Don't fund alone," urges a recent guide to so-called "modern" grantmaking, subtitled *A Guide for Funders Who Believe Better Is Possible*.[2] No foundation by itself can bring about change in a deep-rooted or complex social issue. It is only possible to do so if a foundation agrees to collaborate with others. Collaboration at its most basic will help advance a funder's understanding of the issues through conversations and exposure to the work of others. Collaboration at its most advanced will augment the financial resources and the effort funders can put toward finding solutions. Collaboration with community partners can also help to shift the power between funders and the organizations they work with, as I discussed in Chapter 5.

The type of collaboration I describe in this chapter is not simply an informal agreement to work on a problem together, but a more structured one that can be described as a formal partnership. These partnerships can be with other funders, civil society organizations, businesses, and even governments. They can start informally and become much more formal. Or they can be part of an explicit strategy to extend funds and influence. In some cases, a partnership strategy is the goal itself. Its objective is to build networks and structures for collaboration where none existed before. These partnerships go beyond agreements to pool funds or to co-fund, toward setting goals and working on them together. While this is not typical behaviour for most foundations, foundations that want to create or enter partnerships are motivated by an interest shared with others in "going farther" to solve a particularly complex problem or to move toward a better solution. Indeed, partnerships can lead to real innovations in practice through the combination of resources and skills. They can also be very demanding since they require negotiation, compromise, and communication if they are going to be more than simple co-funding arrangements. Foundation managers need to use specific skills to manage partnerships effectively.

In this chapter I tell the stories of three Canadian foundations that have used partnership approaches to amplify the impact of their work. The Graham Boeckh Foundation works on building integrated youth mental health services across Canada and globally. The Helderleigh Foundation promotes food and media literacy to children in Canada. The Azrieli Foundation partners with organizations across a range of areas, including education, research, the arts, and architecture. All three are structuring partnerships as an approach to increasing their effectiveness and to broaden their reach. Their partnership work has evolved over time as each experience has led to new opportunities.

The Graham Boeckh Foundation

How did Tony and Ian Boeckh come to the decision to strike a formal partnership with a government research funding agency not known for its connections to family philanthropy? Ian suggests that his father's entrepreneurial curiosity was what led them to their first major partnership. The Boeckhs were committed to making a difference for young people like Graham Boeckh, who had struggled to get help from a fragmented health system. Young people, not researchers, were at the heart of their search for answers. And young people needed to be able to access services under one roof: "integrated" youth services. Before he got to this answer, Tony Boeckh asked a lot of questions. "He got to know people, experts at the [CIHR]," says Ian. "[In 2012] he convened a group to give them a Grand Challenge. ... If you had $25 million, what would you do with it to fix youth mental health?"[3] The CIHR was ready. It had committed to a strategy for patient-oriented research in 2011. Under this strategy, the patients themselves (and their families) are proactive partners at the centre of the discussion about health and have a say in shaping health research. Joining forces and committing funds of $12.5 million each, the Boeckh Foundation and the CIHR created a new partnership, Transformational Research in Adolescent Mental Health (TRAM). Together, over a five-year period, the foundation and the CIHR planned to "build and fund one unique pan-Canadian research-to-practice network. This network would unite patients, family members, policy makers, researchers, service providers, community organizations and other stakeholders to move innovative interventions, practices, therapies, or policies out of the research environment and into common use in the real world. More specifically, the network was meant to catalyze fundamental change in youth mental health care in Canada."[4] And youth were going to be at the table.

The plan succeeded to a remarkable degree in kick-starting a Canada-wide push for more integrated youth mental health services. TRAM's challenge led to the formation of a new network, ACCESS Open Minds, which now offers over fifteen sites across Canada where young people from the ages of eleven to twenty-five can go to get the help they need under one roof, including mental, physical, and sexual health services as well as other social services. ACCESS Open Minds is a network that involves youth themselves at the heart, working with families and care givers, service providers, researchers, and policy decision-makers. The network is designed so the different sites can share data and learnings and meet regularly to exchange ideas. The foundation's interest in building networks, breaking silos, and accelerating learning about integrated services was reflected in the design of the process that led to the selection of ACCESS, with close attention paid to bringing together the teams competing for funding so all could gain insight, even if not all were awarded funding.

By 2020, the Boeckh Foundation's partnership with the CIHR to create ACCESS had triggered the formation of similar networks within provinces. For example, in 2015, Boeckh made a proposal to the Government of British Columbia for a project to set up five sites providing integrated services for young people. This public-philanthropic partnership led to the creation of Foundry, a network of sites offering integrated youth mental health services across British Columbia. Foundry aspires to expand to about fifty communities in British Columbia, complemented by services offered through a Virtual Foundry. Boeckh's original funding to create Foundry has been supplemented by millions of dollars in donations from corporate and individual philanthropy in British Columbia. This model has been copied and expanded across the country with many new integrated youth services sites being developed across provinces. "A whole system of language and tools has been developed and adopted [by the foundation and its partners]," says Ian Boeckh. "We learned as we moved from province to province ... now we have a bigger role in creating an ecosystem [for integrated youth services]. We want to engage the federal government in funding knowledge transfer to create a framework for integrated youth services (IYS) across the country."

The decade of investment by the Boeckh Foundation has seen astonishing results. "We would never have guessed at the beginning that this would happen so rapidly," confesses Ian Boeckh. The Boeckh Foundation is not large. It does not have an endowment and is funded annually by contributions from the Boeckh family. But the direct and sustained involvement of two generations of the family and their relentless focus on what youth want and need has created a rapidly evolving movement around IYS in Canada. Ian Boeckh notes how important it is to engage young people directly: "The end point is to help youth. So, if you want to help them you have to talk to them about how they can be helped. They have to be part of the solution. And they are agents of change themselves. The projects are collaborative. Youth collaborate on their own care, on designing the programs ... all are collaborators." He believes the language of collaboration is magical for all partners. The Boeckh philosophy of philanthropy is to treat people respectfully. "We want people to focus on the end point in working together. ... We need different abilities and skills to work together. Carers, researchers, funders, patients, governments. It's not about shifting power but sharing power. You achieve the goals, make decisions, manage the projects together." Ian Boeckh points to two more key factors in making philanthropic partnership work: flexibility and patience. "We realized from the start that we could not achieve our goals without collaborating with government. When we interact with [the public sector partners] we see ourselves as helping them to solve problems. We can do things that they can't. They can do things that we can't. We have found that working in multiple provinces has been helpful ... we are not tied to any one regime. We find early adopters in government, and we are patient. ... You can develop innovations in one province and share them across provinces. This can be very powerful."

"What we have done to develop and spread IYS is to enunciate principles," he concludes. "We don't tell people what to do. We suggest principles around which there is emerging consensus for effective youth mental health care. We discuss principles with partners and collaborators ... how they can be used and adapted in local context. ... Can we agree on what principles are good for families or society and then how can we go there together?" For the Boeckhs, it is more important to care about the outcome of helping young people and their families than to claim ownership or control of projects. "We knew intuitively that using principles would be a respectful and locally responsive way to get a conversation going."

The Boeckh Foundation continues to use its partnership approach to extend its impact. In March 2020, it announced a partnership with Bell Canada through the Bell Let's Talk initiative, with the partners jointly committing $10 million to accelerate the launch of new provincial and territorial IYS projects; help develop, evaluate, and roll out evidence-based innovations in treatment and care to fill existing gaps; and support collaboration across provincial and territorial projects to build capacity and knowledge-sharing. Not content to work simply one-to-one as funders, Boeckh and Bell are working with other Canadian funders in youth mental health through a funder collaborative, the Mental Health and Wellness Affinity Group, which meets regularly to exchange ideas. And on a global scale, Boeckh has nurtured an International Alliance of Mental Health

Research Funders, which connects over thirty funding organizations to increase the impact of mental health research investments. Just as it did within Canada, the foundation is working to stimulate global collaboration, knowing it is crucially important to leverage individual efforts to increase their impact beyond what each funder could achieve on their own.

The Helderleigh Foundation

In 2001, Llewellyn Smith sold his family-owned firm. After four generations, E.D. Smith &. Sons Limited, a food producer based in southern Ontario and a well-known brand across Canada, would no longer be family-owned. But Llewellyn, great-grandson of the firm's founder, Ernest, had grown up around the cultivation and production of fruit and he was passionate about good food. He and his wife, Susan, who is from the medical field, translated this passion into a family foundation, the Helderleigh Foundation, named after the family's former nursery business and home in the Niagara Peninsula. Helderleigh's purpose made it a unique private foundation in Canada, one devoted entirely to building food literacy and better health for children and young families.

Initially the Smiths re-invested in the family fruit farm, which was not part of the company sale. They hoped to educate people about Niagara fruit and fruit production through a charity, the Niagara Fruit Institute. Through their first decade of operation, from 2002 to 2012, the Smiths and the Helderleigh Foundation learned first-hand about the difficulties of growing and marketing fruit, and about the issues of food waste and food insecurity in Canada. In 2012, after disappointing efforts to work with food banks as an answer to food insecurity, they shut down the Niagara Fruit Institute and paused to reflect on where the foundation could be of most value. One of their advisers at the time suggested they consider finding ideas that their philanthropy could help bring to the next level. Her advice was to "jump off the diving board, take some risks and get involved." The Smiths took this to heart. They were committed to confronting the problem of poor nutrition. But they came to two important conclusions: First, if they wanted to make a greater difference, they needed to seek out and support innovations in approaches to education around better nutrition, and, second, they had to do this with partners who could help take innovations to scale. Based on these learnings, the Smiths committed the Helderleigh Foundation to a philanthropic partnership strategy.

In 2013, Llewellyn and Susan Smith were visiting George Brown College in Toronto, a college of applied arts and technology with a culinary school ranked among the top ten in North America. The college was already focused on supporting students interested in entrepreneurship in food innovation and research. But it had minimal engagement in the non-profit space. This gave the Smiths an idea. Could the college help to improve the diet and wellness of people in Ontario by partnering with other non-profits, such as hospitals, health agencies, municipalities, and universities? George Brown was interested in the possibility. Together, Helderleigh and the college as partners agreed to offer a Helderleigh Nutrition Application Fund to support innovative nutrition-related applied research. Twelve projects were funded with ten different non-profit partners, all of which delivered on some aspect of nutrition literacy.

Lorraine Trottier, the dean of the Centre for Hospitality and Culinary Arts, saw a further possibility. Working with Helderleigh, the college could advance students' culinary skills and make them more appealing to employers. The college and Helderleigh realized that the faculty and students could influence and educate more people about the importance of good nutrition behaviours. The two partners signed a multi-year agreement to help bridge the gap between nutrition science and the culinary arts. The curriculum and lab school offerings were updated. Scholarships and nutrition symposia were funded. An investment was made in the professional development of college faculty, which helped them take on a leadership role in driving more change. In 2018, a second agreement was signed expanding nutrition application and awareness in other divisions of the college. These investments by Helderleigh will have a long-lasting impact, preparing students with greater knowledge of nutrition as they enter careers in food preparation and delivery.

Helderleigh's partnership model opened more possibilities for using nutrition to improve people's lives. By 2018, the Smiths and their board began to focus on the importance of nutrition in preventing the development of chronic health conditions. Helderleigh realized it needed to think more about intervening at the earliest stages of life when children are developing the nutrition awareness and habits that will lead to or prevent more chronic health problems much later in life. Llewellyn, Susan, and their board colleagues systematically investigated the most effective opportunities for intervention. With the help of researchers and consultants, they conducted landscape scans and discussed gaps and opportunities with professionals in nutrition, health, and education. As they pursued these conversations, they clarified their approach: They would focus on promoting food literacy for children, their parents, and caregivers. The foundation moved relatively quickly to sign formal agreements with nine partner organizations, including their existing partner, George Brown College, and two universities, several non-profit associations, and a social enterprise. Among them, these partners worked across several areas important to building food literacy, such as developing open knowledge hubs; expanding communities of content experts to influence policy; researching what works in the food literacy field; training educators, intermediaries, and parents; and running "living laboratories" in the field. The foundation characterized its own role as being "a catalyst for bringing experts together, helping translate theory into practice, and advancing policies for a healthier food environment."

Helderleigh was proactive in searching out its partners. Once it identified them, it worked to connect them to each other, much as the Boeckh Foundation does in the mental health field, in the belief that they can amplify each other's work and impact. Helderleigh, like Boeckh, has communicated openly about its approach and its work, hoping to interest other private funders in the work of food literacy. Yet there are challenges to the partnership approach, as the Smiths acknowledge. It is hands-on work. Each of the partners has a different organizational culture and operational practice. "We have learned that [some of the people and partners] we support can be fiercely proud and protective of their work," notes Llewellyn Smith. "Funders come and go. [Partners] are resistant to funders who 'tell them what to do.' ... [But] this is a different deal here ... we are philanthropists rolling up our sleeves, wanting to work with them, bringing their networks and ideas to others."[5] Helderleigh is not an arms-length funder. For each of its formal partnerships, it wanted to set up an advisory council comprising members of the Helderleigh board as well as project partners. Helderleigh board members, many of whom have professional expertise in the nutrition field, could also be advisers. "Our board is engaged, and part of the process," says Smith. "It allows them to provide their input and to give feedback." For many of the partners, however, this was unusual and took them out of their usual practices. They were not used to working with a funder that remained committed to an active collaboration beyond the provision of funding.

An important challenge to a philanthropic partnership approach is the time and skill set required to build trust. "Not everyone wants to work closely ... but we need to work together, learn together," notes Smith. Helderleigh wanted to work with partners who could accept that spirit of collaboration and not keep funders away from the design and implementation of their programs. "It's a matter of making them comfortable ... helping them not to avoid change," says Smith. "We have had to educate ourselves and them on best practices in knowledge dissemination ... we have tried to build the needed strengths on our board to help with execution." These have been significant commitments for a small foundation that has had to manage relationships with partners who were not always prepared to meet the foundation on shared ground. In late 2021, the Smiths and the foundation board decided to conclude their work in food literacy and move the foundation's assets to a donor-advised fund, directed by Charitable Gift Funds Canada Foundation.

Nevertheless, the Smiths agree that the personal time invested in their philanthropic work was immensely valuable to them. For the Smiths, as with the Boeckhs, their work was not about prestige or recognition. Llewellyn Smith concludes "It should be about learning, partnering, collaborating. ... We think that foundations play an important role in doing the work that others are not willing or able to do. It is our role to bring actors together. [Foundations] can bring a different dimension to the work."

The Azrieli Foundation

Naomi Azrieli has an unusual combination of professional experience in asset and investment management and scholarly work in European history. Growing up in Montreal as the daughter of an immigrant who had fled the Holocaust, she developed a personal and professional interest in the twentieth-century history of Europe, which led her to a doctorate at Oxford University and an academic career lecturing at several Canadian universities. She had never imagined herself as the leader of one of the largest foundations in Canada. But she and her father, David Azrieli, who had been a teacher in his early life, shared a passion for education. The family foundation David Azrieli created and named after his family in 1989 became an important funder of students, learners, and educators in Canada and in Israel. In the last decade of his life, David Azrieli drew his daughter into philanthropy as a full-time career while he worked with her to shape his own philanthropic vision and legacy. He was not born into wealth. After immigrating to Canada in 1954, he had built a successful career as a builder and real estate developer. Naomi recalls that her family's culture as she grew up was one of private generosity and commitment to community. But in the 2000s, when David Azrieli was in his eighties, he took some important decisions about philanthropy. To achieve the impact he envisioned, he decided the foundation needed to go beyond making grants and branch out into operations. The Azrieli Foundation's first three operating programs, says Naomi, "scaffolded all the rest that followed."

All three programs had a broad, shared purpose of furthering education. And they were all shaped as collaborations between the foundation and partners. The initial program, launched in 2002, was the Azrieli Institute for Educational Empowerment, which later became the Azrieli Empowerment Program. Initially partnered with the Rashi Foundation and, more recently, with the Darca Schools network, the program, which operates in Israel, focuses on keeping vulnerable young people in formal education. After assessing the ecosystem of initiatives supporting school perseverance in Canada, the foundation took a different approach and provided capacity-building grants to two Canadian organizations: YouthFusion/ FusionJeunesse and Pathways to Education. Each of these organizations was on the cusp of moving from regional to national programming and the foundation's support was intended to further that development. So, while not strictly a formal partnership, these grants were offered to the organizations in the spirit of achieving mutual goals. The second formal partnership program, launched in 2007, was the Holocaust Survivors Memoirs Program, developed and delivered by staff of the foundation to bring the first-person accounts of Holocaust survivors to the public with the goal of educating about the history of the Holocaust. This program partners with local, national, and international institutions of education to achieve its goal. The third was the Azrieli Fellows Program, which funds young researchers, post-docs, and early-career faculty in Israel. The program partners with all of Israel's universities along with the government's Council for Higher Education.

The foundation crafted its education programming by collaborating with educational institutions and organizations that helped the foundation achieve its goals. "Collaborations are always a key element and aim of our philosophy and approach," notes Naomi Azrieli. "We can reach our objectives by collaborating ... not just in funding but also with ideas. Collaboration can also be the objective, not just the means. We look for solutions that have collaborative elements, solutions that bring more people together."[6] All three programs continue to be operated by the foundation, which has broadened the scope of its educational mission by concluding new funding agreements with organizations in Canada and in Israel to educate and empower people at various stages of their lives.

In 2010, David Azrieli took a further step in his philanthropic legacy. He converted the foundation into a public foundation, with a board that included more non-family than family members. Since David Azrieli's death, in 2014, the Azrieli Foundation has grown significantly, with an endowment of well over $2 billion, which makes it one of the largest independent public foundations in Canada. Its focus now extends to scientific research, health care, neurodevelopment, music, architecture, and community support. Education remains at the heart of the foundation's impact, with almost 70 per cent of its investments since 1990 touching on education at the core. And in each area and program, says Naomi Azrieli, they make the effort to find collaborative opportunities for interdisciplinary creativity. "We aim to break down the silos," she says. "It's become part of our signature to get people to work together and to find solutions, knowing that collective action can have greater impact." The foundation has expressed this philosophy clearly on its website: "We believe in productive partnerships with other funders, thought-leaders and stakeholders in academia, government and the private sector who share our goals. Our collaborations are aimed at amplifying the impact of our funding, as well as creating learning opportunities that can improve philanthropic practices and outcomes."[7]

As the Boeckhs and the Smiths learned, this approach involves significant engagement of people. It's not a passive strategy. People are needed to sit down with would-be partners, negotiate agreements, work on goals together, and continue to monitor and evaluate. Whether it's board members, as in the case of the Smiths, or staff, as in the case of the Boeckhs and the Azrielis, partnership strategies involve human resources and skills. Naomi and her sisters Sharon and Danna are involved in the activities of the foundation but much of the work is now done by staff. Naomi, who is the full-time chair and CEO, has focused on building the foundation's management capacity and subject-area expertise over the last five years. "I have empowered my staff to work directly with partners, co-developing initiatives and thinking about measures of impact together," she says. "We are institution-agnostic as much as possible. We look for good ideas, good teams, silo-busting approaches." Embedded in this perspective is the idea that partnerships are not short-term, and that the foundation team will be working for years with partners with whom they have compatibility and who are prepared to collaborate with them on a long-term basis. For this reason, it is as important for the foundation staff to have expertise in the areas in which they are working as it is to find experts and professionals to deliver for them. Naomi Azrieli concludes that the foundation's credibility and legitimacy both rest on bringing knowledge and expertise to the table. "Our staff's expert and in-depth engagement with grantees is what gives us credibility in the areas where we want to catalyze change."

Conclusion

These stories of three very different foundations have a common theme: Partnership is not for the faint of heart. It takes a foundation far beyond the grantmaking role. These foundations are deliberate about the partners they choose because they hope to work closely with them over many years. And they give much more than money to each relationship. Their leaders use active words to describe what they do: catalyze, convene, create, collaborate, challenge. These leaders all admit it has not been a straightforward or easy path. It has taken time for them to develop their strategies. They have had to grow their staff expertise, and build their boards to include non-family directors with relevant knowledge in the areas they work in. All of them say it is not an easy task to measure the outcomes of their partnerships, in most cases because the issues are complex and the outcomes only visible in the long term. But they are unanimous in saying that what they are doing is not ultimately about themselves. As Ian Boeckh says, "This work is not about us, not about what we want or what interests us. It's about how we help society collaborate, share knowledge, find solutions." The lesson for foundations using partnership strategies successfully is that they must learn to be good partners themselves, willing to take time to build trust, find common ground, listen to others, and tend carefully to the relationships they form.

Reconciliation through Relationships

*The Gordon Foundation, the Catherine Donnelly
Foundation, the Indigenous Peoples Resilience Fund*

The question we need philanthropists to answer is whether they would
like to join us in developing decolonized, reciprocal relationships with
Indigenous peoples – not to "help" them because they are "poor and
needy," but rather to strengthen our own ability to realize our potential, so
that we may then make our full contribution to society and to the future
of everyone's children.

Roberta Jamieson

In June of 2015, a group of more than twenty philanthropic foundations and networks came together in Ottawa to sign a *Declaration of
Action*. Their representatives presented this declaration in formal session
and with ceremony to the commissioners of the Truth and Reconciliation
Commission (TRC) at the close of its five-year investigation of the experience and legacy of the Indian residential school system. The philanthropic
organizations pledged as signatories to honour the spirit, intent, and
content of the TRC's 94 Calls to Action and to ensure the philanthropic
community is engaged in the work of reconciliation. They agreed to
learn and remember, to understand, and to acknowledge the tragedy of
the residential school system and its effects on Indigenous communities,
and to participate and act by sharing networks and resources, building
relationships with Indigenous communities, and supporting the TRC's
findings and recommendations. The drafting and presentation of this
declaration was a first formal acknowledgment by the philanthropic
community of its responsibility and obligation to remedy the neglected
work of relationship-building with Indigenous communities in Canada[1].
Since that day in Ottawa in June 2015, over eighty-five philanthropic
and non-profit organizations have signed the declaration. In the long

148 years from Canada's Confederation in 1867 to 2015, there had never been such a formal commitment on the part of philanthropy to the work needed to repair and reconcile relations between Indigenous communities and the newcomer population. Indeed, there had been little or no relationship at all.

Relationship is a critical word in this work. It is essential to the Indigenous world view. And it contains an idea that should be more familiar to philanthropy, which is the idea of reciprocity. Roberta Jamieson, a respected Mohawk leader from the Six Nations of the Grand River Territory, notes that "Reciprocity is the foundation that underpins all our relationships; it is the lens through which we look at all relationships, both human and non-human. Reciprocity is the essence of how we give and receive. It maintains the cycle of life and the sustainability of our people."[2] The idea of reciprocity was also embedded in earlier versions of European Christian philanthropy and in the traditions of Judaism and Islam.[3] These religious traditions viewed philanthropy as a reciprocal action, in which giving and receiving are undertaken as acts of belonging in community. As Paul Vallely, a British writer on the history of philanthropy expresses it, giving is best when it is mutual, when it involves a relationship and a reciprocity between giver and receiver, a mutual recognition and respect of each other's humanity. "Giving involves not simply the donation of money or material goods but a relationship between donor and recipient which is spiritual, reciprocal, communal and inclusive."[4] This is echoed in the words of Jamieson: "At its heart, reciprocity is not about the individual. It is not about 'acting' upon the world, or 'doing' things to it. It is about a relationship that has to be mutual, holistic and concerned about more than one thing."[5]

To be in relationship is to be engaged, to make the effort to understand and to listen attentively, to exchange with each other in mutual respect. This is very far from the standard practice of many philanthropic foundations – arms-length giving through a formal grant application process or through a strategic determination by the foundation alone of its targeted grantees. To be in relationship means that a philanthropic foundation must accept the idea of a collaborative, reciprocal exchange in which both the foundation and the Indigenous community give and accept gifts of knowledge, learning, funds, and opportunities for connection. The relationship is not only about financial support, although this is an important gift that foundations can bring to the table. It is very much about personal contact and communication. For many Indigenous communities, this is achieved by being on the land or in the physical space of the community. It also means taking time to let the relationship develop and build mutual trust. Yet private foundations created and managed by families or donors have been typically constrained in everything required for relationship-building except money. They have not spent the time; been able or willing to travel; understood the history, the ceremony, or the beliefs of Indigenous communities; and done the necessary internal work of self-questioning of unconscious biases and assumptions required for deep relationship-building.

In 2010, five years before the foundations went to Ottawa to make their *Declaration of Action*, the Circle on Philanthropy and Aboriginal Peoples in Canada (the Circle) and the United Way of Winnipeg commissioned a research paper to map appropriate grantmaking models and processes to help guide funders and Indigenous communities in developing their relationships. This was a benchmark for the philanthropic community which previously (with some exceptions) had very little engagement with Indigenous communities. The Circle itself had begun informally in 2006–07 when a small group of staff from both private and public foundations began to have conversations about how to create dialogue between Indigenous communities and non-Indigenous funders. At a gathering on the land outside of Winnipeg in 2008 with Indigenous Elders and leaders, the Circle took shape in a spirit of reciprocity and reconciliation. This dialogue had previously been ad hoc and fragmentary. Even though some individual private foundations, such as The Gordon Foundation, had engaged for several years in work with Indigenous communities, the foundation community more generally was not paying attention. As the Circle pointed out in 2010, "There is little doubt that foundations are not known or poorly understood among Aboriginal communities and organizations, and philanthropy has overall not played a significant role in Indigenous development in Canada."[6] The decade between 2010 and 2020 has seen a leap in awareness, and a new commitment to building relations. In this chapter, I describe the work of private foundations that are signatories to the *Declaration of Action* and are working on their commitments under that declaration to learn the history, understand the context, and build the enduring reciprocal relations with Indigenous communities that will begin to bridge the gap between philanthropy and these communities across Canada.

The Gordon Foundation

The Gordon Foundation was launched in 1965 by Walter and Elizabeth Gordon, and Duncan Gordon, Walter's brother. At the time, the brothers, then in their 50s, had active careers in politics and the accounting profession. Walter Gordon was a major figure in the Liberal Party of Canada of the early 1960s and had served as Minister of Finance. He, his wife, and brother had distinct philanthropic interests that they pursued through grants to public policy institutes, arts, and health-care organizations. The next generation of Gordons, the three children of Walter and Elizabeth, who had joined the foundation board as early as 1970, continued the foundation's commitment to good public policy and to the arts, but imprinted it with their own passions for education; youth; protection of the environment and natural resources, especially water; and, importantly for the future direction of the foundation, the rights and voices of Aboriginal People in the North of Canada. Over the course of fifty years, and particularly in the last two decades, The Gordon Foundation has gone through an evolution from a grantmaking family philanthropy to an operating foundation with an independent board (two Gordon family members are still directors), pursuing focused strategies in two key areas: water management and conservation in the North, and empowerment of Northern and Indigenous Peoples in the development of public policy by and for the North.

The Gordon Foundation's involvement with the North began through its work in the late 1980s and into the 1990s to support the development of the Arctic Council, formalized in 1996 as an intergovernmental body that included the eight countries with territories north of the Arctic Circle and six Indigenous permanent participants. Through the late 1990s, the foundation became increasingly focused in its strategies on the intersection of environmental issues and Indigenous voices and roles across the North. From its early years, it was prepared to fund initiatives that created structures to enable active participation, skills development, and, ultimately, leadership by the Indigenous Peoples of the North, including Inuit and First Nations. In the late 1990s the foundation funded a groundbreaking three-year project to convene twenty-eight Inuit and Cree communities around Hudson Bay and James Bay to share Indigenous ecological knowledge of the region and to articulate their views on the impact of environmental change. In 2001, the foundation funded the engagement of Inuit Elders with knowledge of Inuit culture and law to share with Inuit students in a first Nunavut-based law degree, the Akitsiraq Law School Program, offered through collaboration with the University of Victoria Law School. The foundation was an early supporter of Indigenous-led and land-based education and research, funding a feasibility plan that led to the creation in 2010 of the Dechinta Centre for Research and Learning. In 2010, The Gordon Foundation began a major and ongoing investment in building the public policy skills of Northern people by launching the Jane Glassco Northern Fellowship (named after one of the daughters of Walter and Elizabeth Gordon). The two-year leadership program supports a cohort of young northerners who gather for training, mentoring, and networking. The fellows produce research policy papers, which the foundation helps to disseminate widely. There have been five cohorts of fellows since the program began, producing papers on topics as various as the Canadian judicial system, the Truth and Reconciliation Commission, self-governance, economic and sustainable development, science communication, education, and treaty-making.

In 2017, The Gordon Foundation began to fund an innovative new program, the Northern Policy Hackathon, bringing northerners together to discuss and formulate specific policy recommendations on issues of importance to the North such as food security and housing. The foundation provides funding, convening expertise, research, and promotion of policy recommendations. In a third program innovation, the foundation began in 2019 to organize Treaty Negotiation and Implementation Simulations, in which emerging Indigenous leaders learn about the skills and processes involved in negotiating treaties. In developing each of these initiatives, the foundation has looked for ways to play a role that is unique but also meets an expressed need by the peoples of the North. Sherry Campbell became president of The Gordon Foundation in 2016. Commenting on its approach, she notes that "The foundation has been in the North so long that it is trusted ... people are open and willing to talk about the gaps they see. We are always interested in that unoccupied space where we can do something meaningful."[7] This focus on working to fill the gaps has prompted the foundation to ask questions and to listen to community leaders, governments, and Elders across the North. The listening effort has made it clear that while the knowledge and the lived experience to inform policy work is present already, held in the minds and voices of northerners themselves, there are few opportunities to assemble and to craft their own policy solutions, rather than having to accept policy solutions from southern Canada. The Glassco Fellowships, the Policy Hackathons, and Treaty Simulations are all programmatic efforts funded by the foundation to support and convene northern voices without inserting itself into the policy development process directly. Campbell suggests that "The Glassco Fellowship and the Policy Hackathon ideas came out of the frustration that people feel about policy being made by people in the south for people in the north. ... [Our role is to] step in to support northern voices. ... The challenge is how to braid traditional life with new policy ideas." She confirms that the choice of policy issues on which to work by fellows and hackathon participants is driven by the experience and impact of living on the land. The approach to policy work is very much "place-based, community-based, land-based." The Gordon Foundation's support for convening has provided opportunities for northerners to develop and present their ideas and solutions to government policy makers in the North and to the federal government, which still determines so much in the context of Indigenous northern lives. Campbell is careful to emphasize that the foundation does not advocate or take positions itself. "We bring value through our convenings that people welcome ... as long as they see us as at the table just listening and not directing, we are accepted." The foundation is seen as a funder that is working through Indigenous advisers and Elders, building relations over time. This is essential. In her view, the role is to be present locally and to build local capacity. "[Policy work] has to be led by communities ... that way the thinking is better. It is the best way to be effective."

The Catherine Donnelly Foundation and Healing Through the Land

The Catherine Donnelly Foundation is an unusual private foundation. It was started in 2003 by a group of Catholic religious sisters, the Sisters of Service, and named after the founder of their community, Catherine Donnelly. It describes itself as a lay-religious alliance that supports projects and programs designed to promote social and ecological justice and to engage those that have been overlooked and excluded. It is now essentially a lay charity, although one of the dwindling group of religious sisters still sits on the board of directors as an Honorable Elder. In the twenty years since it was established, the foundation has focused on housing, adult education, and the environment with the purpose of contributing to a more inclusive, just, and sustainable society through its work with partners in each of these areas. From the start, the foundation has seen itself as a collaborator, not simply an arms-length funder. In 2008 it made an important decision to shift a significant portion of its allocation of funds from annual grants to granting in three- to five-year commitments to partners. The aim was to encourage community-led efforts toward more systemic changes, recognizing the long-term nature of these efforts. It also committed to convening and listening to community partners, in the spirit of service of its founders. As Valerie Lemieux, former executive director of the foundation puts it, "One of the drivers of our work is service to others ... we aren't pursuing our own agenda but furthering an agenda of service ... so we ask how we can amplify and create space for communities to do what they know they need to do."[8]

In 2014, the foundation brought together adult educators from Indigenous, women's, labour, newcomer, arts, and cultural organizations to talk about what their communities needed to bring about change. This led to the creation in 2015 of Righting Relations, a community-based and -led network to strengthen the capacity of individuals and organizations to work for social change. Through local circles of adult educators and community organizers, the Righting Relations network convenes dialogues and supports capacity for social and economic literacy work within communities. Righting Relations is now becoming an autonomous non-profit, with a funding commitment from the foundation through to 2025. Valerie Lemieux notes that the work to develop the Righting Relations program began to shift the thinking of the foundation to the need for a new way of conceiving of its work, particularly with Indigenous communities. Some of the local community leaders involved in building Righting Relations were Indigenous women, and their world view opened the eyes of the foundation to the colonial and male-dominated structures that were barriers to closer partnership with Indigenous Peoples. In 2015, the foundation became one of the early signatories to the philanthropic community's *Declaration of Action*. But this step was only the beginning. "We realized that if we wanted to come out of a colonial philanthropic construct we had to think about the Indigenous world view of interconnectedness," concluded Lemieux.

The foundation went on a journey of reflection led by and with Indigenous leaders, including Kris Archie, a Secwepemc and Seme7 woman from Ts'qescen, and leader of the Circle. This work confirmed them in their intention and strategy of creating space for dialogue without asserting power as a non-Indigenous funder. Lemieux and the foundation board recognized that "We needed to build direct relationships with Indigenous-led organizations if we truly wished to decolonize our funding approach." In 2017 they made a five-year commitment to a new initiative, Healing Through the Land, an effort to construct a pan-Canadian, pooled fund designed and managed by Indigenous People themselves in collaboration with funders. The foundation board took time to build reciprocal understanding and trust, beginning with its own self-reflection. Over three years from 2017 to 2019, the foundation convened four meetings with Indigenous leaders, allies, and other funders to create relationships and work through the possibilities for the fund. The participants themselves identified the interconnected needs and priorities of their communities, including culturally appropriate sustainable housing, renewable energy, language and culture revitalization, and localization of food. These conversations were important to the foundation's work of shifting power. As Lemieux puts it, "In moving towards a decolonized approach to philanthropy, the Foundation seeks to promote a power dynamic different from the standard grantor-recipient relationship. We seek initiatives that promote community decision-making and control over community resources."[9]

Valerie Lemieux stepped down as executive director in late 2019. Reflecting on her time at the foundation, she acknowledges that the attempt to construct a new form of philanthropy outside of the colonial systems and power relationships is challenging and there are multiple obstacles, not least the charity regulatory systems that govern and limit the actions of charitable funders in Canada. Nevertheless, she remains optimistic. "We have entered into the Healing Through the Land process hoping to test a decolonized approach to grant design and decision-making processes," she said, "as well as to mobilize knowledge from this learning for the philanthropic sector at large. ... Healing Through the Land is an opportunity to reshape our grantmaking approach, and to find a balance between openness to working differently and creating new collective ways to work together."[10] In 2019, the foundation brought together First Nations, Métis, and Inuit leaders to continue the work of developing a new model for funders to collaborate with Indigenous communities on land-based initiatives. The Indigenous Steering Committee is co-led by Sheila Watt-Cloutier, an Inuit leader, and Miigam'agan, a Mi'kmaq leader, and supported by the Circle. As it develops, the fund's intent is to build up the community of practice around Indigenous land-based programs through regular convenings and face-to-face meetings among grantees and funders. The learning aspect of the fund is an important one for the participating funders who are invited to contribute not only their money but their time to learn and unlearn practices and to commit to decolonizing their grantmaking more broadly. Continuing to follow through on its commitment to providing no-strings-attached funding to First Nations, Inuit, and Métis Peoples working to heal, build hope, and restore social, cultural, and economic capacity in their communities, in 2022, after consulting Indigenous partners and allies, the foundation gifted $1 million to nine Indigenous-led organizations supporting survivors of the residential school system. Consistent with a relationship-based approach, the organizations can use the funds as they see fit with only the expectation of a short oral or written report to the foundation.

The Indigenous Peoples Resilience Fund and the Northern Manitoba Food, Culture and Community Collaborative

Since the signing of the *Declaration of Action*, the philanthropic community in Canada has pursued collaborative funding as a way of putting action to the words and commitments of the signatories. The Catherine Donnelly Foundation's efforts to explore the possibility of a pooled fund designed and led by Indigenous Peoples is one example. Two other examples of this collaborative work between funders and Indigenous Peoples and communities are the Northern Manitoba Food, Culture and Community Collaborative (NMFCCC) and the Indigenous Peoples Resilience Fund (IPRF). Both initiatives offer funders the opportunity to engage with Indigenous communities. The IPRF has gone further down the path of participatory funding, shifting control and resources into community hands, in a similar vision to that of the Healing Through the Land initiative, with decisions and interactions fully among Indigenous Peoples themselves.

The NMFCCC is focused regionally on Manitoba and primarily on issues around food security, food systems, and sovereignty for remote and rural communities, most of which are Indigenous. When it was created in 2013 as a pilot by the Government of Manitoba, it was in part to create a pathway for philanthropy to grow in these communities, both to attract new funders and to build community capacity for writing grant proposals and entering new funding relationships. The NMFCCC is built around values essential to an Indigenous world view, including reciprocity, relationality, and shared learning. Funders, including private foundations such as McConnell, Lawson, Sprott, and Donner, are expected to commit to sharing their funds and their own time to participate in grant application reviews and, just as importantly, to take advantage of opportunities for learning on the land and with the communities. Northern partner communities apply for grants, which are reviewed together by the NMFCCC's staff, the participating funders, northern Indigenous advisers, and volunteer peer reviewers. Granting is decided by consensus. Administratively, the NMFCCC is on a platform hosted by MakeWay, a public charitable foundation. Since 2014, the NMFCCC has channeled more than $750,000 to twenty-six Northern Manitoba communities for projects such as boreal horticulture, northern beekeeping, community chicken coops, community greenhouses, and traditional food programs reconnecting people with country foods.

The benefit of a model such as the NMFCCC for foundations is that it offers a way of stretching the limitations of foundation staff time and knowledge about Indigenous communities. Just as importantly, it offers funders the opportunity for presence on the land, self-reflection, and learning about Indigenous culture and perspectives. Amy Buskirk, one of the two program staff at the Donner Canadian Foundation, commented on her experience as part of the NMFCCC: "The [NMFCCC] supports dozens of communities and food projects ... we could never do this alone. Given our small staff, we couldn't possibly nurture relationships with all these communities. As well, it would be overwhelming for the communities also to engage with many different funders."[11] After visiting a First Nation in Northern Manitoba and meeting with the NMFCCC northern advisers during a learning trip, Amy had a different vision and understanding of the work of building relationships with Indigenous communities. "Historically, a foundation role created privilege and comfort," she notes, "but several times on [my] trip I was intensely uncomfortable ... circles and debriefings and reflections after the trip helped me think about the work in a new and good way."

In 2020, as the negative consequences of the pandemic were becoming increasingly apparent, especially for vulnerable populations and communities, a new philanthropic fund emerged. The difference was that this time it was a fund launched and governed from the first by Indigenous People themselves. The IPRF was created in mid-2020 to support Indigenous communities across Canada with gifts ranging from $5,000 to $30,000, responding to the needs of communities as they dealt with the pandemic and its aftermath. Funded by over twenty public and private foundations, and led and advised by Indigenous Peoples, the IPRF was addressing the urgent need of many small, rural, and remote Indigenous communities for financial support to cope with the health crisis. But it was also seen from the beginning as a long-term instrument intended to contribute to the resilience of Indigenous communities beyond the pandemic. The speed with which the fund came together in the spring of 2020 resulted directly from the pre-existing relationships and trust that had been built among a group of Indigenous partners and foundations in the 2010s. An early case study of the formation of the IPRF, based on interviews with its organizers, noted that a "widespread agreement on the necessity of a fund focused on Indigenous needs existed long before the pandemic."[12] The catalyst for formation was the unprecedented scale of the health emergency and economic shutdown. The case study observes that "Interviewees agree that while the determination and desire to support the development of Indigenous philanthropic infrastructure was present pre-COVID-19, it was not something that could have easily happened before the outbreak. The current crisis has generated a growing sense of urgency and enabled a decade-long conversation to be put into practice in less than a month's time."[13]

The IPRF was pulled together through a collaborative effort by a team of Indigenous leaders. These included Victoria Grant, Teme-Augama Anishinabeg and the first Indigenous board chair of Community Foundations of Canada, and Wanda Brascoupé, Bear Clan, Skarù·rę', Anishinabe, advised by a group of Indigenous leaders with experience in philanthropy. Community Foundations of Canada agreed to act as the initial host for donated funds. Grant and Brascoupé took on the roles of co-team leaders and self-described "helpers." With this, the IPRF took shape rapidly with grants from over ten foundation donor partners, many of whom were signatories to the philanthropic community's *Declaration of Action* and saw their grants to the IPRF as actions taken in partial fulfilment of their commitment. Commenting on how quickly the relationships that underpin the IPRF seem to come together, Bruce Lawson of The Counselling

Foundation of Canada, one of the donors to the IPRF, noted that the preconditions for foundations to engage were already in place before 2020: the awareness created by the Truth and Reconciliation Commission, the commitment to the *Declaration of Action*, and the leadership of philanthropic networks. In his view, "Foundations had normalized and socialized [the idea of putting the responsibility of distributing philanthropic resources into the hands of Indigenous People]."[14]

In its first year, the IPRF distributed over $5 million to Indigenous communities to support the needs the communities identified in the areas of food security and food sovereignty, community mental health and cultural practices, education, and access to technology and connectivity. Grant and Brascoupé explain that their approach is not transactional. "We are high touch. We talk to people on the phone. We take oral applications. The reporting is flexible."[15] They ask the communities simply to tell them what is most needed. "We use an intuitive, emotional, and practical approach to our work with communities," says Brascoupé. "Our mindset is money as medicine for communities, and we support with gifts and bundles. We don't call them grants. These funds are intended to support the brilliance and ingenuity already present in Indigenous communities."

The work of the IPRF is not simply about providing funds. It is about building enduring and real relationships. The funders of the IPRF, all non-Indigenous foundations, come together quarterly to talk about the work with Brascoupé and Grant, and to exchange with each other on what they are learning. All are eager to understand and to build their relationships with each other, with the helpers of the IPRF, and with the communities helped by the IPRF. As Grant puts it, "We see the IPRF as a bridge. We are in service to the funders but also in service to the communities. We open communication between them." This will continue beyond the crisis of the pandemic to the longer-term goal of building relationship and resilience at a community level. Three private foundations, Inspirit, Laidlaw, and Sprott, came forward in June 2021 with unrestricted grants totalling $8.4 million to begin to create an endowment for the IPRF. In announcing this funding, the foundations said they wished to demonstrate their "commitment to walking beside and with the [IPRF] in collective support of Indigenous communities. Transferring capital helps rewrite relationships as a concrete action of reconciliation."[16] Brascoupé and Grant conclude the work is fundamentally about looking forward and building relationship together. They quote the words of George Erasmus, the great Dene leader: "Where community is to be formed, common memory must be created."

Conclusion

This chapter has described the journey toward understanding and reciprocity in the work of philanthropic exchange between Indigenous communities and settler philanthropic organizations. A central theme is the importance of relationship. For any foundation that has signed the *Declaration of Action*, the way to action is through the effort of relationship-building. And in most cases, this requires getting to know and develop relations of trust with Indigenous leaders and communities. Some foundations, such as The Gordon Foundation, are inviting Indigenous leaders on to their boards of directors. The Catherine Donnelly Foundation's work on Healing Through the Land is steered by Indigenous women, as is the IPRF. Some foundations are engaging Indigenous staff members or asking Indigenous consultants to help them think through their strategies and build their networks. In 2021, the Laidlaw Foundation became the first non-Indigenous private foundation to appoint as their new board president an Indigenous leader, Janine Manning, who is Anishnaabe and a member of the Chippewas of Nawash Unceded First Nation (Neyaashiinigmiing). Many foundation donors, boards, and staff members are participating in cultural competency learning sessions, visits to communities, and exchanges with each other to learn about developing internal capacities and strategies. The Circle is an important intermediary in doing this work of convening, advising, and challenging foundations to do their work of reconciliation through relationship.

This is an evolving story. There is still an enormous amount to do. In the decade from 2015 to 2025, it is likely that the Canadian philanthropic community's understanding of the generational work of reconciliation will have changed greatly. More foundations will have understood the need to move beyond learning and arms-length granting to work that is conducted in relation with Indigenous Peoples. In parallel, more Indigenous communities will have developed relationships, knowledge, and experience in practising philanthropic exchange with non-Indigenous partners. As they lead more collaborative and pooled funds, such as

Healing Through the Land and the IPRF, or participate in Indigenous advisory circles and councils, Indigenous People will share this experience within their own communities. As Janine Manning of Laidlaw puts it, "The ways in which we can be more positive in philanthropy is allowing for more trust-based and participatory philanthropy, wherein we not only engage Indigenous folks, communities, and the organizations that serve them, but we follow their lead. We have them build opportunities and review grant applications so that it's community-informed and what community wants, not what settlers think we need."[17]

It will take time. But it is an important contribution that philanthropy in Canada can make. Roberta Jamieson, the eloquent Indigenous leader, believes this work of reciprocal learning holds promise, not only for Canadian philanthropy but even more for Canadians at large. "If Canada is to surmount its historic and continuing injustices to Indigenous communities," she concludes, "we must encourage exercises in which we work together to develop a new vision: a vision of a future where all communities have conditions worthy of Canada and where we become examples of how people from different cultures and origins can work together to create sustainable communities and futures."[18]

10

Why Foundations Matter

Philanthropy is not perfect but nor is it inherently problematic. It is improvable but not illegitimate, and it has value that urgently needs articulating and defending.

Beth Breeze

What do the brief stories I have told in this book tell us about the possibilities and potential of Canadian philanthropy? A constant in the stories is the willingness of these foundations to experiment and learn. I return to the analogy which I suggested in Chapter 1 of foundations as akin to intelligent and curious dolphins. These foundations are far from mysterious giraffes. Their stories suggest that, like dolphins, they communicate frequently and collaborate often in pursuit of mutual goals. They also learn by doing and try to apply their learning to new situations.[1] For these funders, if we want to use a memorable analogy, dolphins are the better choice.

The foundations I have described illustrate among them the functions that Dr Susan Phillips offered as a categorization of the possible roles of grantmaking foundations: discovery, construction, illumination, and co-creation. As I noted in Chapter 2, these roles are oriented toward change. Innovation supports the early stages of a new approach to a social problem. Construction supports the formation of networks and movements and helps to build fields. Illumination stimulates the generation of ideas through research, discussion, and shaping frameworks to solve problems. Co-creation has an activist and policy advocacy function. The foundations profiled in this book, and others whose work I have referenced throughout, can and do play one or more of the four roles listed above. More than half are engaged in activities that fall under the headings of illumination or construction. This suggests that many of them see their role as catalytic, helping to generate new ideas, or as sustaining, helping to grow networks and fields over time. In other words, they are using the unique capacity of private foundations both to take risks and to persist over a period of years.

As I argued in Chapter 1, private foundations create value when they take advantage of their assets: higher risk tolerance and longer time horizons. To do so, they must also retain autonomy to choose where and how to do their work. This autonomy has been respected by governments, although the public regulator rightly sets reporting accountabilities and minimum conditions on the amounts to be disbursed and the nature of philanthropic grantees. No private foundation can or should hoard its assets. And no charitable foundation in Canada may give to grantees or partners that do not fit with its charitable purposes. They have a duty to serve public benefit. Within these rules, charities in Canada are granted operational freedom to set strategies and make choices if those choices are in pursuit of their charitable purposes. And foundations can make even greater use of this freedom given their financial independence. That said, foundations can and should be held to account for what they can do better.

Beth Breeze, professor of philanthropy at the University of Kent in England, has neatly summed up some of the major criticisms of "big" philanthropy in a book-length defence of British and American philanthropy.[2] She cites three major types of criticism. The power critique relates to the undemocratic (and, therefore, supposedly unaccountable) governance of private philanthropy. The effectiveness critique relates to the subjective (and, therefore, supposedly arbitrary) nature of foundation choices. The populist critique relates to the personal attributes of wealth and race (and, therefore, supposedly elitist) character of private philanthropy. If you add these critical views together, it is easy to see why some would think private foundations might do more harm than good.

What can foundations do in response to this criticism? They could simply spend themselves down quickly and hand over their funds to communities. But this would be to abandon the advantages conferred by high risk tolerance, long time horizon, and autonomy of choice. In my view, the best response is to demonstrate value and legitimacy by being as accountable and open as possible, and by being willing to explain their philanthropic choices and to share evidence that the work they fund or do contributes to the improvement of our society. At various points in this book, I have commented on the way in which Canadian foundations are endeavoring to be more transparent, investing in their listening skills, and bringing more perspectives to the table. Could they do more?

Harbingers of Change

I see signs of change in foundation practice on both sides of the Atlantic. The philanthropic conversation in Canada and in Europe, not just in the United States, is focusing on how to make philanthropy more open and more responsive to the community. At a conference of European foundations in Vienna in October 2021, the urgency and scale of societal issues were clearly forcing a questioning of philanthropic practice. According to the European Foundation Centre, the organizer of this conference, foundations in Europe feel the need to find answers to how best to augment their contributions.[3] They are actively debating how to play a role in addressing the overlapping challenges of climate change and social and economic inequality. Regional tensions between western and eastern Europe and particularly rising tensions between autocracies and democracies are also forcing philanthropy to consider more urgently how to strengthen democratic institutions across the continent. Foundations are aware they cannot waste any time in tackling both systemic inequality and the climate emergency. They are thinking about increasing their grants but also doing more radical things to shift resources: issuing debt, transferring capital, and/or spending down their capital strategically. They are acting to change their practices so grants are available more quickly, on more flexible terms, over more years.

Research from the Center for Effective Philanthropy (CEP) in the United States indicates many American foundations are treating the positive changes to granting practices they made during the pandemic as being more than simply temporary. According to a 2021 CEP survey[4] of foundations, almost all the leaders surveyed said they plan to sustain some of the changes they have made in response to the societal challenges of systemic racism and racial inequality that will endure post-pandemic. As the authors of the CEP report note, "It's not an uncommon refrain to hear some within the non-profit sector ask, with exasperation, 'What will it take for foundation philanthropy to change?' The answer appears to be the extraordinary circumstances of a global pandemic and a heightened, long overdue societal discussion of long-standing systemic racial inequities."[5] The CEP researchers observe that their data point to a level of change in foundation practice they have not seen in the two decades they have been conducting research about philanthropy.[6] Phil Buchanan of the CEP noted that "More than a few foundations actually showed their mettle these last two years and, in doing so, made a strong case – if we really analyze what happened – for the unique role that endowed, long time horizon institutions can play in a moment of great crisis … the pandemic arrived at the tail-end of a flurry of high-profile, and often highly generalized and unnuanced, critiques of 'big philanthropy' as somehow inherently illegitimate. In this context, the pandemic, coincidentally, provided foundations a chance to demonstrate why they matter. Many took it – supporting crucial nonprofits with stepped up giving and more trust in them to deploy those resources wisely to help people and communities in a time of great need."[7]

At the same time, foundation leaders acknowledge the need for greater transparency and diversity of thought in their decision-making and governance. And they are agreeing on the need for more and better data and analytical tools to understand their impact and to share what they are learning. This interest in understanding impact does not mean a return to the so-called top-down "strategic" philanthropy of the early 2000s and the data-driven measurement of outcomes that can be attributed to a single foundation. Instead, funders are being encouraged, or, indeed, pushed through their collaborative work to exchange information and evidence with each other about "what works." Interestingly, collaborative networks are functioning not only as ways to lever impact but also as ways for foundations to hold each other accountable. In 2020–21, collective pledges of various kinds were organized, calling on foundations to make a public commitment to act on inequality, equity, or the climate emergency, and to set and meet public targets for their activity. In Canada, research[8] on foundation responses to the health emergency confirm, as similar research did in the United States, that foundations responded quickly in the early stages of the crisis with more funds, distributed to more organizations serving vulnerable populations, with fewer conditions and restrictions. Six months into the crisis, more foundations were increasing their collaboration with each other. A team of Canadian academic researchers who followed a group of twenty-two granting foundations (private and public) over the course of the first year of the pandemic noted that "The pandemic has shown many foundation leaders the significance and value of collaboration in the sector – not only to themselves, but for their communities as well. The past year has also highlighted inequalities and the need to address the root causes of why some communities are often more negatively impacted by major events like this than others. Panelists expressed that they have learned the importance of being flexible and adaptable and that change is sometimes inevitable – something that is easier to face when you are willing to move with the current rather than against it."[9]

As their experience accumulates, foundations may find it easier to set mutually agreed objectives and desired outcomes for which they hold themselves collectively accountable. But as researchers warn, "The path forward for increased impact, relevance and legitimacy will require deep, inclusive, and challenging conversations and continued experimentation."[10] And it will take courage. A demonstration of this courage comes in the form of a collective pledge made public in November 2021 by a group of fifteen public and private foundations in Quebec, the Collectif des fondations québécoises contre les inégalités.[11] This pledge to Quebec society is a commitment to battle inequality in all its forms. The important aspects of the pledge are the clarity of the fundamental principles that the signatories endorse: that foundations play an important role in society that is distinct and complementary to that of the state; and that those foundations need to demonstrate their contribution to the common good by being accountable to the public and by continuing to improve the impact and coherence of their actions. The pledge[12] commits the signatories (which include Quebec-based foundations discussed in this book, such as McConnell, Trottier, Chagnon, and Saputo) to specific actions, including aligning their own internal values and practices to an orientation of "redistribution," adopting practices that will "shift the power" toward their partners – and specifically toward excluded or marginalized groups – and realigning their investments to support work to reduce inequalities. The pledge is backed up by a list of specific actions to undertake, and examples of actions in a summary document prepared by the partner of the collectif, the academic research group PhiLab. It's an unprecedented and detailed philanthropic commitment to making fundamental shifts to previous practices. Many of the signatories have already started to walk along this road as I described in the chapters on strengthening community and shifting power.

No one is saying this will be an easy shift. We know that philanthropic foundations could be better at what they do. They could strengthen their support for their own field infrastructure and networks. They could invest more in their staff capabilities and in their use and sharing of data. They could participate in more systematic learning, and knowledge mobilization, either on their own or though funder collaboratives. They could simplify their processes, reach out more to their communities of interest, and listen better. They could re-allocate more of their funds to historically marginalized and racialized groups. And they could enter situations and conversations where they will be uncomfortable because that is the only way to get to more trusting relationships. The pressure is strong and the agenda for change in philanthropy is clear. Indications are that many foundations are aware and are working on it. As Breeze notes, "There is a deep disjuncture between the worrying about philanthropy that regularly pops up in the media and in public discussions as if no one – including donors – has ever noticed a problem before, and the long-standing, deep commitment of many donors and people working in [the] philanthropy sector to understand, address, and improve their practice … the criticisms have been set out, have been heard, and are being worked on."[13]

The Canadian Difference?

I believe foundations in Canada are in a relatively strong position to respond and even to lead change in philanthropy, and to improve their own effectiveness as agents for change. While I do not want to make an argument for Canadian philanthropic exceptionalism, I think we have certain advantages, not least our ability to connect with each other across what is still a relatively small population. Historically, Canadians have been pragmatists. We have been willing to work with and complement the public sector, not oppose it. This is in part due to the activism of the public sector from the 1960s on and a progressive tilt in our national social and economic policies that has resulted in public education, public health, and social security systems that provide most of our population with a common safety net and opportunities to build good lives. Many, if not all, of the foundations in this book would support this progressive consensus. We are not as polarized by politics or ideology as the philanthropic sector in the United States.[14] And this gives foundations in Canada a good starting point for collaborative effort. One of the striking similarities in the work of so many of the foundations I have described is their role of convenor, calling together different players, reaching across sectoral lines, and creating tables for all to sit at together to find solutions.

On the critical issues of today – climate emergency, inequality, systemic racism, importance of reconciliation – I think Canadian philanthropy has much to offer inside and outside our borders. We live in a country whose economy has depended, in part, on extracting and burning carbon. We have an enormous environmental space at risk, in land, water, and air. Given this, Canadian philanthropists have an opportunity and an obligation to make space for policy development around a sustainable transition, to help generate ideas around carbon pricing and carbon

capture, to help protect and conserve old forests and grasslands, and
to support urban building and transportation strategies to get to the
hugely challenging goal of net zero. We are citizens in a diverse and
pluralist country that has supported a continual flow of immigrants from
many parts of the world over the last twenty-five years. This means that
Canadian philanthropy can work collaboratively and at scale on social
and racial inclusion, and on strategies to strengthen civic engagement and
our institutional and democratic responses to pluralism. And we live in
a country where settlers share the land with the Indigenous Peoples who
are the original inhabitants. This means an opportunity for Canadian
philanthropy to be more creative in integrating Indigenous concepts of
reciprocity and exchange with western philanthropic ideas of community
building and improvement of society. Finally, we are people who have
roots and connections in many countries around the world. Philanthropy
can and should do more to support the global need for better public
health, stronger democracies, and more solid governance.

Is philanthropy in Canada doing these things as well as it could? No.
Our positive Canadian cultural traits can also be weaknesses. Our prag-
matism can lead to caution, our modesty can become lack of aspiration.
And our politeness can become a reticence to speak out publicly and
advocate for social change. Our humility can lend itself less positively
to a lack of will to examine and talk about hard facts in our history and
in our present. Most private foundations are not governed by diverse
boards and that means important voices and perspectives aren't included.
More foundation leaders need to put attention and resources into their
listening and learning and into their public sharing of that learning.
These are all characteristics that can be recognized and changed. What
gives me hope is that the foundations whose work I have described are
led by Canadians who bring the needed traits and skills to the work of
change. I spoke to over thirty staff and board members of foundations
while researching and writing this book. In their stories about how their
foundations have evolved, and about their next steps, they collectively
demonstrated curiosity, balanced by a realistic appreciation of the limits
of what they know. They are modest in a good way. Their philanthropic
work isn't driven by ego but by purpose. They know foundations hold
power and that it should be used with sensitivity, not arrogance. Most
are grappling with how to build relationships that give room to the voices
and perspectives of their grantees and help them think beyond the walls
of their organizations. They live with uncertainty, since they are placing

bets on the future, and doing so without complete control or certainty of success. If there are common characteristics to all these foundations, it is their combination of focus, persistence, acceptance of risk, and openness to new thinking.

The full impact of social change can take many years to achieve. When I think about the decades-long work of the foundations I have profiled in this book, I feel confident in describing them as oriented toward change, not simply charity, although the changes they hope for, and the outcomes they want, are not always measurable. It is not useful to answer the question of why the work of foundations matters to social change simply by adding up numbers of lives saved, families fed, children protected, or people employed. The organizations funded by foundations can certainly track these outcomes. But many indicators of progress toward change are more elusive. They could be in the form of public policies adopted or discarded, or organizations and leaders enriched through networks, or communities learning to do things differently. It is difficult to take stock of such indicators at a single moment in time since a good deal of this change emerges or can be seen only after it has taken place. This does not mean foundations should not try to capture evidence as it emerges. Many of the foundations I have described try to communicate what they have learned as they are learning it, although this is not yet the practice of the majority. What I can say with confidence is there has already been enormous change in the world of Canadian foundations in the twenty years since I began working in the field. Communities themselves are driving this change. The events of recent years have made so much clearer to all of us the overlapping nature of inequality, health, and climate crises, and the effects of historic racism and exclusion. The voices raised to claim social and racial justice cannot be unheard. Communities' calls for change are catalyzing change in the actions and behaviours of philanthropic foundation players. The work foundations have been doing in the last few years to evolve and broaden their strategies, and to share their evidence and insights, helped in some measure to prepare them for the shifts of 2020 and beyond. The many Canadian foundations that are starting up or are engaging new generations of board members and staff leaders are taking inspiration and ideas from different sources, including from the fields of social investing and social entrepreneurship. Philanthropy is already a very different field than it was even a decade ago.

Final Thoughts: Why Do Foundations Matter?

Why do foundations matter? Because they are part of an ecosystem. In a balanced ecosystem, one element depends on and contributes to many others. Take one away and the ecosystem is damaged in unexpected ways. In the ecosystem of philanthropy, long-life private foundations are only some of the actors, joining individual donors, donor-advised funds, giving circles, mutual aid associations, and online giving intermediaries. Giving itself is an action undertaken by many different players and not unique to foundations. But in our broader social ecosystem, long-life foundations contribute many important things beyond grants: knowledge-building, social research and development, network creation and convening, organization and infrastructure support, influence, and advocacy. They act as signals to others around ideas and innovations that will matter not today but maybe five or ten years from today. These contributions can and even should be made with others. What differentiates the foundation contribution is its continuity over time and the ability to give with patience for outcomes that may only be realizable in the long term. Philanthropic investments in designing and testing new social programming, or support for policy development studies, or core support to build networks and develop leaders, must be made and maintained for several years before generating maximum social benefit. Solving our country's most complex challenges will require and depend on the continued investment of risk-tolerant and independent philanthropic capital. Philanthropic resource providers for social change are the must-have elements of the ecosystem we need if our future society is to be both more resilient and more sustainable. The final argument of this book, and its coda, is well expressed by one of the foundation leaders I interviewed:

> In a world where the needs are vast and immediate ... we should be the rare money – the support that is not otherwise available – that opens a door, draws a connection, conjures an opportunity, or creates a pause.
> Sandy Houston, president of the Metcalf Foundation

Notes

Introduction

1 The Lucie et André Chagnon Foundation.
2 Private Foundations Canada, later renamed Philanthropic Foundations Canada (PFC).
3 *Tzedakah* is the Hebrew word for righteousness or justice; *zakat* is a Muslim religious duty to contribute wealth to the poor; *sadaqah* refers in Arabic to the voluntary giving of alms.
4 There are many popular definitions of the meaning of philanthropy. The *Merriam-Webster* dictionary notes the derivation of the word "philanthropy" is from late Latin *philanthropia*; from Greek *philanthrōpía*, from *philanthrōpos* (loving people), from *phil- + anthrōpos* human being. From the same dictionary, the derivation of the word "charity" is from the late Latin *caritas*, or "Christian love."
5 For a detailed historical account of the idea of philanthropy as charity, see Vallely, *Philanthropy from Aristotle to Zuckerberg*.
6 Couchman, Struthers, and Wiebe, "All My Relations," 131.
7 Fong, *J.W. McConnell*, 513.
8 Lefèvre and Elson, "Contextual History," 7.
9 Walker, *From Generosity to Justice*, 19.
10 The Ford Foundation website, https://www.fordfoundation.org.
11 Philanthropic Foundations Canada, *Foundations Seeing the World Differently*.
12 A term used by Matthew Bishop and Michael Green, *Philanthrocapitalism*.
13 Elson, Lefèvre, and Fontan (editors), *Philanthropic Foundations*.

14 Callahan, "Powerless," https://www.insidephilanthropy.com/home/2018/10/9/
    defeat-how-top-foundations-failed-to-stop-the-conservative-march-to-
    powerand-now-risk-losing-everything

Chapter One

 1 Phillips, "Dancing with Giraffes," 151–183.
 2 Designation of private or public depends on the structure, source of funding,
    and governance of a foundation. The *Income Tax Act* differentiates public
    and private foundations by the question of control: Can the foundation be
    controlled by a single individual or group of related individuals? The measure
    for this is whether more than 50 per cent of the individuals on a foundation
    board are not at arms-length from each other. Typically, private foundations
    do not fundraise, depending on an endowment or on funds regularly flowed
    through the foundation by donors.
 3 The full list of registered charities can be found on the CRA website, https://
    www.canada.ca/en/revenue-agency/services/charities-giving/list-charities/list-
    charities-other-qualified-donees.html.
 4 Philanthropic Foundations Canada, Top 150 Foundations by Assets (2018),
    internal PFC data.
 5 "Canadian Foundation Facts," PFC, accessed February 14, 2022.
 6 Philanthropic Foundations Canada, Top 150 Foundations by Assets (2018),
    internal PFC data.
 7 Data on the purposes of grants and descriptions of fields of funding interest are
    not available from the CRA. Data can only be displayed on dollar amounts of
    grants and names of grantees.
 8 "Key Facts On U.S. Nonprofits and Foundations," Candid, April 2020,
    https://www.issuelab.org/resources/36381/36381.pdf.
 9 Statistics Canada Annual Demographic Estimates, https://www150.statcan.
    gc.ca/n1/pub/91-215-x/91-215-x2021001-eng.htm.
10 BMO Wealth Insights, https://www.bmo.com/assets/pdfs/wealth/wealth-
    insights--emagazine-wealth-connects-the-generations--Issue01-cdn--en.pdf.
11 Statistics Canada Economic Well-being Across Generations of Young
    Canadians, 2019, https://www150.statcan.gc.ca/n1/pub/11-626-x/11-626-
    x2019006-eng.htm.
12 Mehta and Johnston, "Diaspora Philanthropy and Civic Engagement in
    Canada," 10.
13 Investor Economics and TD Wealth, *Time, Treasure, Talent*.
14 Ibid., 28.
15 Ibid., 21.

16 Funk, *Doing Good for Business*.
17 Rockefeller Philanthropy Advisors and Campden Wealth Limited, *Global Trends and Strategic Time Horizons*, 19.
18 Williamson and Leat, "Playing Piggy(bank) in the Middle," https://doi.org/10.1111/1467-8500.12461.
19 Ford Foundation, *Annual Report 1966*, https://www.fordfoundation.org/media/2436/1966-annual-report.pdf.
20 Hutchins, "The Argument for Mandatory Payout is Misguided," https://web.archive.org/web/20161102004055/http:/www.acf.org.uk/news/the-argument-for-mandatory-pay-out-is-misguided.
21 Fleishman, *The Foundation*, 16.
22 Brodhead, "Grantmaking Leadership."

Chapter Two

1 Buchanan, *Giving Done Right*, 60.
2 Phillips, "Dancing with Giraffes," 167.
3 Buchanan, *Giving Done Right*, 87.
4 Phillips, "Dancing with Giraffes," 175.
5 Soskis, "Norms and Narratives," https://www.urban.org/research/publication/norms-and-narratives-shape-us-charitable-and-philanthropic-giving.
6 Kania, Kramer, and Russell, "Strategic Philanthropy for a Complex World."
7 Porter and Kramer, "Philanthropy's New Agenda."
8 Ibid.
9 Kania, Kramer, and Russell, "Strategic Philanthropy for a Complex World."
10 Buchanan, *Giving Done Right*, 89.
11 Ibid., 105.
12 Phillips, "Dancing With Giraffes," 157.
13 Reich, *Just Giving*, 161.
14 Ibid., 165.
15 Ibid., 193.
16 Ibid., 163.
17 Ibid., 191.
18 Lefèvre and Elson, "A Contextual History," 13.
19 Ibid., 14.
20 Unwin, "Provocations," https://socialinnovationexchange.org/insights/provocations-living-turbulent-times-and-recentring-conversation.
21 Northcott, interview with the author, November 30, 2020.
22 Buchanan, *Giving Done Right*, 192.

Chapter Three

1 Rodin, "Philanthropy as Field Builder," https://www.rockefellerfoundation.org/blog/philanthropy-as-field-builder/.
2 Ibid.
3 Farnham, Nothmann, Tamaki, and Daniels, *Field Building*.
4 Ibid., 10.
5 Ibid., 7.
6 Bruce Lawson, interview with the author, November 25, 2020.
7 The Counselling Foundation of Canada, 2020 Strategic Plan, https://counselling.foundation/mission-vision-values-guiding-principle/.
8 Ibid, 2.
9 Marcel Lauzière, interview with the author, November 3, 2020.
10 Farnham, *Field Building*, 11.
11 Sadia Zaman, interview with the author, January 12, 2022.
12 For more on the remarkable achievements of Vibrant Communities and Tamarack, see *Helping Communities Change: The 15 Year Tamarack Story* https://www.tamarackcommunity.ca/hubfs/Tamarack%202030%20Future%20Search/2017%2015%20year%20history.pdf.
13 Brodhead, "Comments to Meeting."
14 McConnell exceeded this target with 15 per cent of its portfolio invested for impact at the end of 2020.
15 Pearson, *Accelerating Our Impact*, 48.
16 Ibid., 52.

Chapter Four

1 Metcalf Foundation mission statement, https://metcalffoundation.com/about/#overview.
2 Definition provided by Coady International Institute, St Francis Xavier University.
3 Phillips, "The New Place of Place."
4 Sandy Houston, interview with the author, November 3 and 15, 2020.
5 B-Corporations are defined as companies that meet high standards of social and environmental performance, accountability, and transparency. B-Corporations are certified by B Lab, a US-based non-profit organization.
6 Pole and Berube, "Centraide's Collective Impact Project."
7 Ibid., 270.
8 Ibid., 279.
9 Murphy, "Community Wealth Building."

10 The Ontario Employment Education and Research Centre provides public
    education and awareness on workplace legislation and workers' rights. The
    ACORN Institute provides leadership training for low-income neighbourhoods
    and for worker and civic engagement in work and employment policy issues in
    Toronto and nationally.

11 Atkinson Foundation website, https://atkinsonfoundation.ca/atkinson-fellows/.

12 Colette Murphy and Jenn Miller, interview with the author, November 15,
    2021.

13 Ibid.

14 Pole and Berube, "Centraide's Collective Impact Project," 279.

Chapter Five

1   Heimans and Timms, *New Power*, 8.

2   Soskis, *Norms and Narratives*.

3   Ibid.

4   The latter reason is a good rationale for participating in pooled or collaborative
    funds run by or advised by members of communities served by the grants.
    Examples of these participatory pooled funds are described in chapters 5 and 9.

5   Wrobel and Massey, *Letting Go*, 32.

6   "Arnstein's Ladder of Citizen Participation," *The Citizen's Handbook*, retrieved
    on August 6, 2021, https://www.citizenshandbook.org/arnsteinsladder.html.

7   Wrobel and Massey, *Letting Go*, 146.

8   Chouinard and Lagarde, "Becoming a Part of Quebec's Social Fabric."

9   Ibid.

10 Jean-Marc Chouinard, interview with the author, October 22 and
    November 23, 2020.

11 Chouinard and Lagarde, "Becoming a Part of Quebec's Social Fabric."

12 Chagnon Foundation, "Sondage sur la perception des acteurs sociaux,
    https://fondationchagnon.org/la-fondation/publications/sondage-perception-
    fondation-chagnon-2021/.

13 Jehad Aliweiwi, interview with the author, December 14, 2020.

14 Ibid.

15 Dupre, "Centring Indigenous Youth Leadership."

16 Jehad Aliweiwi interview. December 14, 2020.

17 Laura Manning, interview with the author, February 1, 2021.

18 Lyle S. Hallman Foundation website, https://www.lshallmanfdn.org.

19 Laura Manning interview. February 1, 2021.

20 Ibid.

21 Ibid.

22 Liadsky, Taylor, Coffman, Beer, and Lopez, *Approaches to Learning Amid Crises*, 16.
23 Liadsky, Taylor, Coffman, and Lopez, *What It Takes to Learn During Crises*, https://taylornewberry.ca/what-it-takes-to-learn-during-crises-reflections/

Chapter Six

1   Ideas That Matter, http://www.ideasthatmatter.com/aboutus/index.html.
2   Gibbins, "The Moral Imperative for Policy Advocacy," https://thephilanthropist.ca/2016/02/the-moral-imperative-for-policy-advocacy/.
3   Ibid.
4   Many more examples of foundations engaging in a variety of ways in policy work are provided by Marcel Lauziere in his chapter "A Lever for Change" in *Intersections and Innovations*.
5   The work of The Gordon Foundation is described in more detail in Chapter 9.
6   Elizabeth McIsaac, interview with the author, May 14, 2021.
7   TRIEC remained a program of Maytree until 2012 when it became an independent non-profit.
8   Allan Northcott, interview with the author, November 30, 2020.
9   Northcott, "Reflections on Teaching Public Policy Advocacy Skills."
10 A similar training program was later seeded by Max Bell in British Columbia under the sponsorship of the United Way of the Lower Mainland.
11 Allan Northcott, interview with the author. November 30, 2020.
12 Bob Wyatt, interview with the author, December 14, 2020.
13 Ibid.
14 Davies, *Public Good by Private Means*, 206.

Chapter Seven

1   Sparrow, "Firms must justify investment in fossil fuels, https://www.theguardian.com/business/2019/dec/30/firms-must-justify-investment-in-fossil-fuels-warns-mark-carney.
2   Ivey Foundation *Annual Report 2014*, https://www.ivey.org/wp-content/uploads/2020/02/IVEY-AR-2014.pdf.
3   Ivey Foundation *Annual Report 2015*, http://www.ivey.org/wp-content/uploads/2019/11/IVEY_AR_2015_WEB_VARIANT_FINAL.pdf.
4   Bruce Lourie, interview with the author, October 2, 2020.
5   Ivey Foundation *Annual Report 2019*, https://www.ivey.org/wp-content/uploads/2020/06/Ivey-AR-2019-R9-final.pdf.
6   Ibid.

7   Ivey Foundation annual reports, https://www.ivey.org/reports-2/.
8   Donner Canadian Foundation website, retrieved July 4, 2021. https://www.
    donnerfoundation.org/granting.htm.
9   Helen Maclean, interview with the author, April 19, 2021.
10 Trottier Family Foundation website, https://www.trottierfoundation.com/
    about.
11 Sylvie Trottier, interview with the author, October 2, 2020.
12 c40 is a global network of large cities committed to addressing climate change.
    Montreal, Toronto, and Vancouver are members.
13 Federation of Canadian Municipalities, "Meet lc3's Climate Leaders" series,
    retrieved from https://fcm.ca/en/resources/article-series-meet-lc3-climate-leaders.
14 Ibid.
15 Montreal Climate Partnership media release December 10, 2020, https://
    climatmontreal.com/en/lancement-du-partenariat-climat-montreal/
16 Eric St-Pierre, interview with the author, September 11, 2020.
17 Sylvie Trottier, interview with the author. October 3, 2020.
18 Roeyer, Hamad, Fox, and Menon, *Funding Trends*, https://www.climateworks.
    org/report/funding-trends-climate-change-mitigation-philanthropy/.
19 Dunsky Energy Consulting. *Building Canada's Low Carbon Future*,
    (Environment Funders Canada, 2020), 37.

Chapter Eight

1   Ian Boeckh, interview with the author, October 21, 2020.
2   Bull and Steinberg, *Modern Grantmaking*.
3   Boeckh, interview with the author. October 21, 2020.
4   Canadian Institutes of Health Research, *Building Strength*, (CIHR and Graham
    Boeckh Foundation, 2020), 3.
5   Llewellyn and Susan Smith, interview with the author, January 18 and 20, 2021.
6   Naomi Azrieli, interview with the author, February 18, 2021.
7   Azrieli Foundation website, https://azrielifoundation.org/how-we-work/.

Chapter Nine

1   Indigenous is used in this chapter to refer to First Nations, Inuit, and Métis
    Peoples and communities.
2   Jamieson, "Decolonizing Philanthropy," 160.
3   Noted by Vallely in his lengthy analysis of the history of western philanthropy,
    Philanthropy from Aristotle to Zuckerberg.
4   Ibid., 113.

5   Jamieson, "Decolonizing Philanthropy," 162.
6   AMR Consulting, Aboriginal Philanthropy in Canada, (United Way of Winnipeg, 2011), 16.
7   Sherry Campbell, interview with the author, February 9, 2021.
8   Valerie Lemieux, interview with the author, July 20, 2021.
9   Catherine Donnelly Foundation, "Healing Through the Land," 28.
10 Ibid., 30.
11 Amy Buskirk, interview with the author, April 30, 2021.
12 Isidora Sidorovska, Indigenous Peoples Resilience Fund, 3. Retrieved from https://philab.uqam.ca/wp-content/uploads/2020/11/Indigenous_FINAL_2.pdf.
13 Ibid.
14 Bruce Lawson, interview with the author, November 25, 2020.
15 Wanda Brascoupé and Victoria Grant, interview with the author, February 11, 2022.
16 Community Foundations of Canada, "Leading Canadian Foundations Increase Investments," https://communityfoundations.ca/press-release-leading-canadian-foundations-increase-investments-to-advance-reconciliation/.
17 Morriseau, "Indigenous Folks Have Always Been Philanthropists"
18 Jamieson, "Decolonizing Philanthropy," 169.

Chapter Ten

1   For more on dolphins as learners, see https://www.sciencedaily.com/releases/2020/06/200625115929.htm.
2   Breeze, In Defence of Philanthropy.
3   McQueen, "The Future of Philanthropy in Europe," https://www.alliancemagazine.org/conf-report/alliance-webinar-future-of-philanthropy-in-europe/.
4   Buteau, Orensten, and Marotta, Foundations Respond to Crisis.
5   Ibid., 28.
6   Ibid., 28.
7   Buchanan, "Two Years Later, Part Two," https://cep.org/two-years-later-part-two-who-trusted-and-why-it-matters/
8   Philanthropic Foundations Canada, "Philanthropy Responds to COVID-19, 3rd Report," https://pfc.ca/wp-content/uploads/2022/03/pfc-covid-survey-report-november-2020_final.pdf.
9   Phillips, Raggo, Pue, and Mathieson, "Foundations During COVID-19 Panel," 10, https://pfc.ca/wp-content/uploads/2022/03/session-6-foundations-during-covid-july.pdf.
10 Ibid., 8.

11 The collectif des fondations came together at the end of 2014 and includes
    Quebec-based public and private foundations and charities.
12 https://www.collectifdesfondations.org/déclaration-dengagement.
13 Breeze, *In Defence of Philanthropy*, 145.
14 Many foundations have conservative or neutral views on social and economic
    policy questions or, simply through their funding choices, support established
    institutions and traditional charities. These foundations do not intend to
    change systems. Their contribution as funders is valued by charities and by
    communities and not to be underestimated. But their choices are not apolitical.
    Philanthropic foundations exercise power through their funding decisions,
    and this means they are political actors. Even the smallest foundations can be
    subject to the critique of elitism and should be mindful of the importance of
    demonstrating accountability and a degree of transparency.

Bibliography

AMR Planning and Consulting. *Aboriginal Philanthropy in Canada: A Foundation for Understanding*. United Way of Winnipeg 2011.

Bishop, M. and M. Green. *Philanthrocapitalism: How the Rich Can Save the World*. London: A&C Black, 2008.

Breeze, Beth. *In Defence of Philanthropy*. Newcastle upon Tyne: Agenda Publishing, 2021.

Brodhead, Tim. "Comments to Meeting of Foundation Partners." *Reflections on Philanthropy and Society: The Speeches of Tim Brodhead*. Montreal: The J.W. McConnell Family Foundation, 2011.

– "Grantmaking Leadership." *Reflections on Philanthropy and Society: The Speeches of Tim Brodhead*. Montreal: The J.W. McConnell Family Foundation, 2011.

– *In A World of Unpredictable Change, What Canada Needs Most is Resilience*. Montreal: The J.W. McConnell Family Foundation, 2011.

Buchanan, Phil. *Giving Done Right: Effective Philanthropy and Making Every Dollar Count*. New York: PublicAffairs, 2019.

– "Two Years Later, Part Two: Who Trusted and Why It Matters," April 12, 2022, https://cep.org/two-years-later-part-two-who-trusted-and-why-it-matters

Bull, Gemma and Tom Steinberg. *Modern Grantmaking: A Guide for Funders Who Believe Better Is Possible*. London: Modern Grantmaking, 2021.

Buteau, E., N. Orensten, and S. Marotta. *Foundations Respond to Crisis: Lasting Change?* Cambridge, MA: Center for Effective Philanthropy, 2021.

Callahan, David. "Powerless: How Top Foundations Failed to Defend Their Values – and Now Risk Losing Everything." *Inside Philanthropy*, October 9, 2018.

Canadian Institutes of Health Research. *Building Strength: Transformational Research in Adolescent Mental Health*, 2020.

The Catherine Donnelly Foundation. "Healing Through the Land: Navigating Philanthropy's Role in Reconciliation – A Funder's Journey." *The Philanthropic Year*, Volume 2, Winter 2020, PhiLab.

Chouinard, Jean-Marc and F. Lagarde. "Becoming a Part of Quebec's Social Fabric: Lessons from the Chagnon Foundation's Growth Trajectory 2000–2018." *The Philanthropist*, February 4, 2019.

Couchman, Stephen, M. Struthers, and J. Wiebe. "All My Relations: A Journey of Reciprocity." In *Philanthropic Foundations in Canada: Landscapes, Indigenous Perspectives and Pathways to Change*, edited by Elson, Lefevre, Fontan. Victoria: Tellwell Talent, 2020.

Davies, Rhodri. *Public Good by Private Means: How Philanthropy Shapes Britain*. London: Alliance Publishing Trust, 2016.

Dunsky Energy Consulting. *Building Canada's Low Carbon Future: Opportunities for the Philanthropic Sector*. Environment Funders Canada, 2020.

DuPré, Lindsay. "Centring Indigenous Youth Leadership in Reconciliation Philanthropy: Promising Practices at the Laidlaw Foundation." *The Philanthropist*, February 19, 2018.

Elson, Peter, S. Lefèvre, and J-M Fontan, editors. *Philanthropic Foundations in Canada: Landscapes, Indigenous Perspectives and Pathways to Change*. Victoria: Tellwell Talent 2020.

Farnham, L., E. Nothmann, Z. Tamaki, and C. Daniels. *Field Building for Population-Level Change*. The Bridgespan Group, March 2020.

Fleishman, Joel. *The Foundation: A Great American Secret; How Private Wealth is Changing the World*. New York: PublicAffairs, 2009.

Fong, William. *J. W. McConnell: Financier, Philanthropist, Patriot*. Montreal and Kingston: McGill-Queen's University Press, 2008.

Funk, Carla. *Doing Good for Business: The Inclusion of Philanthropy in the Canadian Professional Advisor's Business Practice*. Canadian Association of Gift Planners, 2018.

Gibbins, Roger. "The Moral Imperative for Policy Advocacy." *The Philanthropist*, February 1, 2016, https://thephilanthropist.ca/2016/02/the-moral-imperative-for-policy-advocacy/.

Goulet, Liza and S. Hoang. *Snapshot of Foundation Giving in Canada in 2018 and Trends 2013–2018*. Philanthropic Foundations Canada, 2021.

Heimans, Jeremy and H. Timms. *New Power: How Power Works in our Hyperconnected World – and How to Make It Work for You*. Toronto: Random House Canada, 2018.

Hutchins, Emma, "The argument for mandatory payout is misguided." Association of Charitable Foundations, October 20, 2016 (archived website).

https://web.archive.org/web/20161102004055/http:/www.acf.org.uk/news/
the-argument-for-mandatory-pay-out-is-misguided.

Investor Economics and TD Wealth, *Time, Treasure, Talent: Canadian Women
and Philanthropy*, Addendum, May 2016.

Jamieson, Roberta. "Decolonizing Philanthropy: Building New Relations."
*Philanthropic Foundations in Canada: Landscapes, Indigenous Perspectives and
Pathways to Change*, edited by Elson, Lefèvre, and Fontan. Victoria: Tellwell
Talent, 2020.

Kania, J., M. Kramer, and P. Russell. "Strategic Philanthropy for a Complex
World." *Stanford Social Innovation Review*, Summer 2014.

Lefèvre, Sylvain, and P. Elson. "A Contextual History of Foundations in
Canada." *Philanthropic Foundations in Canada: Landscapes, Indigenous
Perspectives and Pathways to Change*, Victoria: Tellwell Talent, 2020.

Liadsky, B., A. Taylor, J. Coffman, T. Beer, and A. Lopez. *Approaches to
Learning Amid Crises: Reflections from Philanthropy*. Center for Evaluation
Innovation and Taylor Newberry Consulting, 2020. https://taylornewberry.
ca/wp-content/uploads/2021/03/Approaches-to-Learning-Amid-Crises.pdf.

Liadsky, B., A. Taylor, J. Coffman and A. Lopez. "What It Takes to Learn
During Crises: Reflections." Blog post. Taylor Newberry Consulting.
Retrieved August 31, 2021. https://taylornewberry.ca/what-it-takes-to-learn-
during-crises-reflections/.

McQueen, Annmarie. "Conference Report: Future of Philanthropy in Europe,"
Alliance Magazine, October 26, 2021. https://www.alliancemagazine.org/
conf-report/alliance-webinar-future-of-philanthropy-in-europe/.

Mehta, Krishan and P. Johnston. "Diaspora Philanthropy and Civic
Engagement in Canada: Setting the Stage." *The Philanthropist* 24. No. 1
(2011).

Morriseau, Mike. "Indigenous Folks Have Always Been Philanthropists: A
Conversation with Janine Manning." *The Philanthropist*, November 2, 2021.

Murphy, Colette. "Community Wealth Building: A Canadian Philanthropist's
Perspective." In *Intersections and Innovations: Change for Canada's Voluntary
and Nonprofit Sector*, edited by Susan D. Phillips and Bob Wyatt. Edmonton,
AB, Canada: Muttart Foundation, 2021.

Northcott, Allan. "Reflections on Teaching Public Policy Advocacy Skills." In
*Intersections and Innovations: Change for Canada's Voluntary and Nonprofit
Sector*, edited by Susan D. Phillips and Bob Wyatt. Edmonton, AB, Canada:
Muttart Foundation, 2021.

Pearson, Katharine A. *Accelerating Our Impact: Philanthropy, Innovation and
Social Change*. The J.W. McConnell Foundation, 2007.

Philanthropic Foundations Canada. *Foundations Seeing the World Differently*.
PFC, 2003 (out of print).

– *Philanthropy Responds to* COVID-19, *3rd Report* COVID-19 *Data Mapping Series*. November 2020. https://pfc.ca/wp-content/uploads/2022/03/pfc-covid-survey-report-november-2020_final.pdf.

Phillips, Susan D. "Dancing with Giraffes: Why Philanthropy Matters for Public Management." *Canadian Public Administration*, 61(2) (2018): 151–83.

– "*The New Place of Place in Philanthropy: Community Foundations and the Community Wealth-Building Movement.*" Paper presented at the International Society for Third Sector Research (ISTR) conference, Amsterdam, July 2018.

Phillips, Susan D. and B. Wyatt (editors). *Intersections and Innovations: Change for Canada's Voluntary and Nonprofit Sector*. Edmonton, AB, Canada: Muttart Foundation, 2021.

Phillips, S., P. Raggo, K. Pue and C. Mathieson. *Foundations During* COVID-19 *Panel, No.6*, Philanthropy and Nonprofit Leadership, Carleton University, July 20, 2021. https://pfc.ca/wp-content/uploads/2021/08/session-6-foundations-during-covid-july.pdf.

Pole, Nancy and M. Berube. "Centraide's Collective Impact Project: Poverty Reduction in Montreal." In *Philanthropic Foundations in Canada: Landscapes, Indigenous Perspectives and Pathways to Change*, edited by Elson, Lefèvre, Fontan. Victoria: Tellwell Talent, 2020

Porter, Michael and M. Kramer. "Philanthropy's New Agenda: Creating Value." *Harvard Business Review*, November–December 1999.

Reich, R. *Just Giving: Why Philanthropy Is Failing Democracy and How It Can Do Better*. Princeton: Princeton University Press, 2018.

Rockefeller Philanthropy Advisors and Campden Wealth Limited. *Global Trends and Strategic Time Horizons in Family Philanthropy 2020*. https://www.rockpa.org/wp-content/uploads/2020/01/Global-Trends-and-Strategic-Time-Horizons-in-Family-Philanthropy_FINAL.pdf.

Rodin, Judith. *Philanthropy as Field Builder*. Rockefeller Foundation, April 25, 2013. https://www.rockefellerfoundation.org/blog/philanthropy-as-field-builder/.

Roeyer, Hannah, M. Hamad, M. Fox, and S. Menon. *Funding Trends: Climate Change Mitigation Philanthropy*. ClimateWorks Foundation 2020. https://www.climateworks.org/report/funding-trends-climate-change-mitigation-philanthropy/.

Sidorovska, Isidora. *Indigenous Peoples Resilience Fund: Building Infrastructure for Indigenous Philanthropy*. PhiLab, July 2020. Retrieved from https://philab.uqam.ca/wp-content/uploads/2020/11/Indigenous_FINAL_2.pdf.

Soskis, Ben. *Norms and Narratives That Shape US Charitable and Philanthropic Giving*. The Urban Institute, March 4, 2021. https://www.urban.org/research/publication/norms-and-narratives-shape-us-charitable-and-philanthropic-giving.

Unwin, Dame Julia. "Provocations: Living in Turbulent Times and Recentring the Conversation." Social Innovation Exchange, September 11, 2020. https://socialinnovationexchange.org/insights/provocations-living-turbulent-times-and-recentring-conversation.

Vallely, Paul. *Philanthropy: from Aristotle to Zuckerberg*. London: Bloomsbury Publishing, 2020.

Walker, Darren. *From Generosity to Justice*. Ford Foundation, 2019.

Williamson, A. and D. Leat. "Playing Piggy(bank) in the Middle: Philanthropic Foundations' Roles as Intermediaries." *Australian Journal of Public Administration*, February 17, 2021.

Wrobel, Ben and Meg Massey. *Letting Go: How Philanthropists and Impact Investors Can Do the Most Good by Giving Up Control*. Published independently, 2021.

Zaman, Sadia. "*Inspirit: Fostering Reconciliation and Building Trust with Indigenous Communities*." PANL Carleton University, November 22, 2021.

Index